"In *Dynamics of Marriage*, Jack Dominian has given us a carefully crafted, clinically accurate, user-friendly gem. Couples, engaged or married, will find here enough challenge and practical explanation of what happens in love to ponder over and over. Read the book once and then be prepared to go back and study it, because it won't let go of you."

Larry Losoncy, Ph.D.
Marriage and Family Therapist
Tulsa, Oklahoma

"Whatever happened to Christian marriage? This book will provide an honest, unsparing, yet ultimately hopeful answer to married couples and counselors alike. Through historical and psychological developments and contemporary Christian teaching, Dominian provides a holistic and promising vision of marriage today.

"Especially helpful is his advocacy of the theory that early life in the family shapes how, as adults, we love and commit ourselves as marriage partners. His position, rooted in traditional psychiatric theory and contemporary Christian belief, is that it is possible to grow and to change as human beings, and to build marriage through affirmation, forgiveness, and 'never-ending healing.'

"This book offers meaning and a message that begs to be heard!"

Valerie Vance Dillon
Author and Family Life Educator

"Dominian, speaking from a wealth of experience and careful study, steps back and looks at marriage from a sociological viewpoint. There is no moralizing, just thoughtful investigation of the shifts in marriage today, the causes behind its new, and not so new, difficulties, and careful insights on ways to enable marriage to become a healing partnership. *Dynamics of Marriage* should be read by all counselors, pastors, teachers, and parents who are concerned with family and who influence the lives of those preparing for marriage."

Kathleen Chesto
Author, *Family Spirituality*

"*Dynamics of Marriage* is a remarkable look at how important marriage is to the world and to the church. This is one of those rare books that actually offers new ideas and insights into marriage, which theologian Karl Rahner called 'the smallest...genuine individual Church.' Married couples who read this book will gain a deeper appreciation for their vocation; those who minister to married couples will gain a deeper appreciation for what they are about."

Mitch Finley
Author, *Christian Families in the Real World*

DYNAMICS *of* MARRIAGE

Love, Sex, and Growth from a Christian Perspective

JACK DOMINIAN

TWENTY-THIRD PUBLICATIONS
Mystic, Connecticut 06355

Acknowledgment

The Scripture quotations are taken from the *New Jerusalem Bible* published and copyright 1985 by Darton, Longman and Todd Ltd. and Doubleday & Co., Inc.

North American Edition 1993

Originally published in England by Darton, Longman and Todd, © 1991 by Jack Dominian, as *Passionate and Compassionate Love: A Vision for Christian Marriage.*

Twenty-Third Publications
185 Willow Street
P.O. Box 180
Mystic, CT 06355
(203) 536-2611
800-321-0411

ISBN 0-89622-563-1
Library of Congress Catalog Card Number 93-60137

Printed in the U.S.A.

Preface

At the heart of this book there are three themes: 1) the understanding of marriage as a community of love, 2) that it is through this love that the overwhelming majority of human beings find God, and 3) that sexuality and love are linked in a vital way.

1. Today we are in the midst of a social revolution in which marriage is shifting from a traditional "form," which has prevailed for the last hundred years, to a relationship of love. This secular shift, which is hard to detect because we are in the middle of it, is coinciding with a religious view that also treats marriage and the family as a community of love. There is thus the challenge of reconciling the two approaches so that society and the Christian community can engage in a common venture.

2. It is important for the church to recognize that marriage is the principal way through which the majority of human beings experience God, in so far as God is love. There is a deep sense of urgency for Christianity to put marriage on the map, and to show that in this community of love God is to be found.

3. Coupled with a reinforcement of the significance of marriage, we need to restore the unique importance of sexuality. Sexuality has had poor treatment at the hands of Christianity for the whole of its duration. Sex was made respectable only by linking it to procreation. Today the overwhelming majority of sexual activity is non-procreative, and a new meaning has to be found for this precious gift from God.

You will note that there are no references in this book. The reason is that, while the book is based extensively on research findings and my own clinical observations, it has not been written as a scientific document. I want as many people as possible to read *Dynamics of Marriage* unburdened by the clutter of scientific references.

Jack Dominian

Contents

1

The Centrality of Love

For most of us one of the central experiences of our life is our childhood, during which we received the essentials of love. For nearly two decades we were dependent for our survival and development on our parents. Modern psychology is in the process of analyzing this period, and it is discovering that the secret of life is to be found in a combination of the genes with which we were endowed and the experiences we shared with our parents. It is no exaggeration to state that these two decades unfold for us the mystery of life, and this mystery is to be found in one word, love. This love is experienced in the first relationship of intimacy in our childhood. Courtship and marriage bring us into a second exclusive attachment of intimacy. Thus love experienced in and through intimacy links our childhood with our adult life.

At the heart of the Christian faith is the centrality of love, and one of the purposes of this book is to show that marital love constitutes for most human beings their central experience of God. Their most precious neighbor is first their spouse, then their children, and finally the neighbor who is near or far away. There is a great danger in contemporary society to miss this point. It is missed by the secular world which sees marriage as a mere contract with social implications. It is missed by Christianity which recognizes marriage as a sacrament, but does very little to help Christians see its vital importance in their life. The secular world can be forgiven for mistaking marriage for a mere contract, but even here we shall see that it is moving in the direction of appreciating the importance of love. But Christianity has no excuse, for love has featured centrally in its revelation throughout the Judeo-Christian tradition. It will be argued by critics of this view that the love of the Scriptures, particularly of the New Testament, is that of *agape*, not *eros*. But this is a false distinction because, as we shall see, marital love encompasses both falling in love and loving. Marital love is love of neighbor, and scriptural love is also love of neighbor.

Love of neighbor is to be found in the law of Moses, the essentials of which are written in the Book of Leviticus:

> When you reap the harvest of your land, you will not reap to the very edges of the field, nor will you gather the gleanings of the harvest, nor will you strip your vineyard bare, nor pick up the fallen grapes. You will leave them for the poor and the stranger. I am Yahweh your God. You will not steal, nor deal deceitfully or fraudulently with your fellow-citizen. You will not swear by my name with

the intent to deceive and thus profane the name of your God. I am Yahweh. You will not exploit or rob another. You will not keep the laborer's wage until next morning.... You will not harbor hatred for your brother...You will not exact vengeance on, or bear any sort of grudge against, the members of your race, but will love your neighbor as yourself. I am Yahweh (Leviticus 19:9–18).

Jesus picks up where Leviticus leaves off:

And now a lawyer stood up and, to test him, asked, "Master, what must I do to inherit eternal life?" He said to him, "What is written in the Law? What is your reading of it?" He replied, "You must love the Lord your God with all your heart, with all your soul, and with all your strength, and with all your mind, and your neighbor as yourself." Jesus said to him, "You have answered right; do this and life is yours" (Luke 10:25–28).

But the lawyer wanted to be clever, and he asked Jesus the difficult question, that is, "Who is my neighbor?" He received the majestic reply that has reverberated through the centuries, the story of the Good Samaritan.

In the Johannine gospel we have one of the most powerful pronouncements of love:

This is my commandment: love one another, as I have loved you. No one can have greater love than to lay down his life for his friends (John 15:12–13).

And in his epistle, he gives us the ultimate significance of love:

My dear friends, let us love each other, since love is from God, and everyone who loves is a child of God and knows God. Whoever fails to love does not know God, because God is love (1 John 4:7–8).

God is love, and love of neighbor is the summation of all Christian teaching. In marriage two people vow to love one another for life, and in the vicissitudes of this love they encounter God in each other:

No one has ever seen God, but as long as we love each other, God remains in us and God's love comes to its perfection in us (1 John 4:12).

God is the unseen and the unknown force that holds the world together, and in the process holds each one of us. God does this in and through love. As long as we are loving, we are in God's presence, and God is in us. In fact we love many people, but the person we love most constantly is our spouse. Every moment is a choice for or against loving him or her. So marriage is the central sacrament of love through which we find God. This does not mean that those who are single, separated, divorced, unloved, cannot find God, or are not in the presence of God—everyone has their way of being in the presence of God—but it does mean that for married couples God is to be found continuously in the neighbor/spouse and in their children. In the presence of this love the invisible God becomes visible. Because love is so vital in a marriage, I will next explain in great detail what it is and how it affects the dynamics of a marriage.

2

What Is Love?

&

There is no one agreed-upon definition of love. Is it the thrill of the chase? Is it the excitement of being in close proximity to the beloved? Is it the pleasure of sex and sexual intercourse? Or is it the moment-to-moment pleasure of being involved with, sharing, and doing things for someone who matters? Love can be all of these things, and each of these moments can be exciting.

In this chapter I will present the "evolutionary" view of love which holds that all of these moments taken together are meant to lead to the generation of offspring, who will in turn have children themselves. In order to have children people need to find a mate, and the first process of love concerns sexual attraction. Men and women have different needs when it comes to sexual attraction. Men seek attractive women who have qualities of beauty, age, and health. This is all bound up with eroticism. Traditionally Christianity has been frightened of the erotic, but in an evolutionary sense it is the background that supplies the energy to the subsequent union. Men seek physical beauty. Women are also attracted by male beauty, but even more important they need qualities that ensure security for the subsequent needs of the child. Thus women would be influenced by evidence of money, possessions, status, ambition, and industry. The evolutionary model encourages female attractiveness and male stability which will encourage sexual intercourse and fertilization and provision for the helpless infant. While exterior qualities are influential, the final choice of a mate requires social and psychological aptness in addition to erotic and material suitability. A good marriage needs more than beauty and money. Couples have to retain interest in one another. They have to stimulate, encourage, support, excite, and fire each other's imagination, but the base design in the evolutionary view is of perpetual attraction and social stability.

Need for Exclusivity

Having obtained a partner, the next requirement of the evolutionary model is for exclusivity. Exclusivity is another word for ensuring that the couple raise their own children and remain available for their nurturing. The two threats to exclusivity are infidelity and the disappearance of a spouse. The infidelity of a wife endangers her to a pregnancy, and the risk that the husband will be asked to raise someone else's children. Even the occasional act of infidelity on the part of a woman used to risk a pregnancy in the days before effective contraceptives, hence the long and universal importance of fidelity. Male infidelity meant that he could impregnate another woman, and re-direct resources from his own family to the raising of other children. Fidelity nowadays is important because in the prevailing intimacy of the couple, infidelity is an act of disloyalty and betrayal which undermines trust.

The next factor is the preservation of the spouses to ensure the nurturing of the children. In the past, death was the single most important danger to parental presence. Today marital breakdown and divorce have become the most common reason for parental departure.

Thus the selection of a partner and the subsequent exclusive relationship within marriage form the background to love. Within marriage erotic attraction leads to sexual intercourse for the purposes of procreation. When infant mortality was high and the duration of life short, sexual intercourse was largely, or almost exclusively, concerned with procreation. Today, with advances in medicine, the reduction of family size, and the advent of contraception, the majority of sexual intercourse is non-reproductive and is channeled toward strengthening the bond of the couple. The intense excitation of erotic arousal and sexual pleasure tend to concentrate and associate love with sexual activity. In the evolutionary model, the erotic component is primarily at the service of fertilization, the meeting of ovum and sperm.

Once children are produced they must be fed, nurtured, protected, taught, and loved. This is the final consequence of the evolutionary model: the love of parents for their children that evokes acts of intense heroism and the quiet and persistent efforts over two decades by parents to give their children their best. The love required by the parents to stay together to nurture their children and the consequent parental love are the least obtrusive but most powerful tokens of love. At the heart of this aspect of love is staying in relationship, and it reflects the divine characteristic of the Trinitarian ability to stay in a loving relationship for eternity.

Six Broad Goals

In this evolutionary view of love, there are six broad goals. These are display or attractiveness, exclusivity, commitment, marriage, sexual intimacy, reproduction, and parenting. The evolutionary approach to love suggests that "love acts" have evolved to serve these goals because of their consequences of reproductive success. What is needed, however, is an understanding of how mate selection is achieved. What is the mechanism by which two people become bonded to each other?

Still situated within the evolutionary model, we have the work of John Bowlby which has thrown light on infant attachment. His work is based on ethology, and he has shown that infants become attached to their mother within a few days to weeks from the time of their birth. This attachment is based on vision, sound, touch, and smell. The baby, first in a limited way, and then increasingly more strongly, recognizes visually first the face and then other parts of the mother's body. Her voice becomes a familiar sound and, of course, the sensations of touch give the baby a sense of security.

Through these physical means and the sense of smell, the baby forms an affective attachment, that is to say, it is emotionally bonded to the mother and therefore wants to stay by her side. If the young child wakes up and finds mother missing, or indeed if mother is absent for any reason, her physical disappearance leads to a sequence of behaviors. First, there is protest which involves crying, and this is followed by searching which can go on for days. If the search is fruitless, it leads to despair, a state of passivity and sadness. Finally there is detachment, in which the bond is broken, and, if the mother returns after a long period, the baby ignores her. This sequence can also be seen when we lose touch with someone we love, and it is the pattern of loss for any reason.

From Cradle to Grave

Bowlby suggests that attachment behavior characterizes human behavior from the cradle to the grave. It is particularly pertinent to that stage of falling in love whereby a particular man or woman becomes the exclusive object of our love. There are many similarities between the attachment of the infant (AI) and a lovers' attachment (LA).

Both AI and LA are reciprocal. The mother responds to her baby's needs, and lovers are mutually aware of each other. This reciprocity causes both the baby and the lovers to feel safe, confident, and secure. When the mother or lover is not available, then the infant and the lover become anxious, preoccupied, unable to concentrate. The infant and mother spend a good deal of time holding, touching, caressing, kissing, smiling, clinging to each other, and so do lovers. When infant and lovers are sick, worried, threatened in any respect, they like to be held and soothed by their mother and the beloved. Both experience distress at separation, searching for the missing mother or lover, and finding no peace until there is a reunion. When reunion takes place, there is intense joy.

Although the baby can be attached to more than one person, such as its father, grandmother, or siblings, there is usually one key person, normally the mother. Lovers have other friends, but they love one special person who exhibits feelings of jealousy when attention is diverted from him or her. There is a great deal of non-verbal communication between mother and baby, and also primitive verbal sounds of cooing. Lovers also coo, talk baby language, and use non-verbal communication. This simple but highly effective communication is coupled with an intense awareness of the infant's inner world by the mother. Lovers show the same degree of mutual awareness of each other's inner world, and that is called empathy.

In further work on Bowlby's theories, it has been shown that the attachment of infants can be divided into three categories: secure, anxious, and avoidant. As far as the secure infant is concerned, it believes and acts as if the mother is accessible, even when she is out of sight. The anxious baby cries more than the secure baby, clings to its mother more, and cannot use her as a safe base from which to explore its environment. The avoidant baby tries to escape the gaze, contact, and intimacy of its mother.

Research has shown that these three types of attachment can be found in adults.

In a secure attachment, it is relatively easy to get close to others, to feel comfortable depending on them, and in turn to be depended upon. Such a person rarely feels the threat of being abandoned. One who has an anxious attachment wants almost to merge with the partner and fears not being loved or wanted. An avoidant attachment is one in which a person feels uncomfortable being close to others and finds it difficult to trust or be dependent on others, or to allow them to get too close. It has been found that secure attachments form about 50 percent of all attachments; anxious about 25 percent; and avoidant about 25 percent.

This description of these three attachment types is associated with certain personality features. Secure people consider themselves easy to get to know and likable, and they feel that other people are generally well intentioned and goodhearted. Anxious people have more self-doubts, feel misunderstood and underappreciated, and trust others less. The avoidant person falls between these two categories.

Attachment theory shows that we are equipped genetically to form attachments from the time we are born till the time we die. This ability allows us to form an exclusive relationship with a man or a woman, and enter into the intimate partnership of marriage. It does not tell us, of course, why we choose a particular person, but, when we do make a choice, our behavior becomes intimate and passionate.

Ten Signs of Intimacy

When a choice has been made, warmth is established between a couple that is expressed in intimacy. These signs of intimacy have been identified: desiring to promote the welfare of the loved ones, experiencing happiness with them, having high regard for them, being able to count on them in times of need, having mutual understanding, sharing oneself and possessions, receiving emotional support, giving mutual support, having intimate communication, and valuing them in one's life.

Within the context of this intimacy, passion is expressed in terms of romance, physical attraction, and sexual consummation. In most instances sexuality is the main component of passion, but other needs, such as self-esteem, dominance over others, submission, and self-actualization, may be prominent features.

In this chapter I have made an attempt to portray love on a scientific basis, from an "evolutionary" view. The foundations of love are the attraction necessary to bring men and women together to mate and maintain the race. The particular mechanism of attachment forms the specific basis of bonding within the overall evolutionary force. Attachment brings a couple together, and intimacy and passion maintain the attachment.

Disorders of love emerge from this outline when the human acts which lead to attraction and courtship are separated from commitment, leading to casual relationships or, after commitment, to infidelity. Within the orbit of attachment, it can be seen that anxious and avoidant personalities have difficulties with their intimacy requirements, needing either too much or too little from their partners.

This group of disorders does not by any means exhaust the various distortions of love, but it gives an outline of how to examine difficulties associated with love.

In the next chapter I will examine love from a different viewpoint, namely the experience we all have as children.

3

Childhood Experiences of Love

For nearly everyone the first experiences of love are associated with childhood. As we grow up and consider adult patterns of behavior as the norm, we tend to ignore our childhood. In fact we spend a great deal of time and effort making sure that we are not seen to behave in childish ways. We try to control impulses for immediate gratification, and we cope with pain and adversity without running to the nearest parent figure. What we forget is that the foundations of love are learned in childhood, and it is to these that we revert when we relax in the intimacy of loving relationships. In order to understand the nature of our intimacy expectations, we have to understand the deep layers of our childhood experiences.

Affective Attachment Is Formed

As already mentioned in the previous chapter, the first critical step of expressing love begins when we form an affective attachment to our mother in the first few weeks of life. We do this through vision, sound, touch, and smell. We begin to recognize slowly first her face, with its various features, and then the rest of the body. We learn to respond to her smiles and frowns, and in this way we get the first glimpse of approval and disapproval. The same thing happens with her voice. We become attuned to its various inflections, from affirmation to severity. The voice gives information about her physical whereabouts, and it forms a radar system of communication with her. It is a means of constant reassurance when she cannot be seen. The most powerful stimulus, however, comes from touch. Holding and being held signal strong affectionate sensations in which the baby feels safe, wanted, and appreciated. This is also the way to obtain comfort when distress is experienced in the form of physical pain or any form of anxiety. In the depths of the arms of mother we are fed both physically and emotionally.

This affective bonding is first experienced with mother, and then in time with father, brother, sister, and grandparents. The attachment forms a protective network for the infant, and it gives all of us our first experience of love. If one observes the interaction between a mother or father and their baby, there is a reciprocal rhythm of bodily contact, smiling and talking to each other. Thus the foundations of love are laid down in the context of bodily encounter, a feature to which adults will return throughout their life in their loving moments, emotionally and sexually. Whenever we fall in love or make a deep friendship, we form an affective attachment. We are attracted by another's appearance, the sound of their voice, and we want to be in their physical presence and hold them. Thus attachment, as we have seen, is basic to loving, and when we lose the people we love we are sad, cry, and mourn their departure, just as an infant cries at the absence of the key figures in its life.

Learning to Trust

Within the physical bonding just described, children learn the rudiments of trust. Trust is experienced physically, emotionally, and intellectually. Physical trust is conveyed through feeling safe and comfortable in the presence of the key attachment figure. Safety and comfort are experienced by a relaxed sensation in the presence of the other person. The security continues throughout life, and is felt when we are in the presence of people we recognize as friendly or close to us. Children are totally dependent on their parents and other adults for safety, hence the revulsion that is felt when they are physically, emotionally, or sexually abused.

As we grow older the signals of trust are conveyed emotionally. We receive messages of trust by the way people smile approvingly, greet, or affirm us. All these signals give us the feeling of being wanted and approved, and they become the basis for our interaction with other people. These signals test the atmosphere of trust between people.

As we grow older we are able to relate to others cognitively as well as physically and emotionally. As we begin to understand language and deal in it, trustworthiness is expressed in veracity. We need to believe what people say to us, and in turn they need to believe in us. Hence the importance of truth. That is why it is so important that we treat our children with the greatest care in respect to truth. Very soon, by the age of three, they will develop sharp memories and insights into what we have told them, and they will remind us without the slightest hesitation when we contradict ourselves.

I cannot exaggerate the importance of trust in all human dealings, particularly in intimate relationships. In
these we are offering our bodies, minds, and hearts to another person. We need to be able to trust them as completely as possible. In sexual intercourse we reveal our
naked bodies, which become the instruments of loving
mutuality. In conversation we express our deepest
thoughts, the truths we have reached by hard work, and
we want them to be treated with care and respect, even if
the other does not agree with them. In our loving exchange we bestow our deepest investment of affection on
another, and we desire an equivalent reciprocity. It is essential for intimacy that we trust the people closest to us
to be reliable. It is this reliability that gives us the basis of
trust in the rest of our lives.

Steps Toward Autonomy

Within the context of this secure trust, a child begins
to separate from mother and father. Initially it will crawl
a few yards away and then return to the safety of a parent's presence. This behavior has been compared to a ball
to which an elastic has been attached. The elastic is the
child that stretches itself for increasingly longer distances,
but then it flies back to the ball. Thus the child learns to
explore its surroundings and to discover new things for
itself.

Slowly the child acquires the skill to walk, dress, feed
itself, and talk. In all these respects it is acquiring autonomy. This is the first stage in life when we learn the balance between closeness and separateness. For increasingly
longer periods, the child will cope by itself, playing on its
own or with other children, away from the key parental
figure, and then it will return to its base. In psychological
terms, it is learning to internalize, to keep the parent's
presence alive inside in her or his physical absence.

The same thing applies to adult friendship or love. We spend a lot of time with the person we love, but we also have to spend time apart. When we are with those we love we feel a great deal of pleasure. The degree of distress we experience in their absence depends upon how much they matter to us and how well we have internalized them. When we have them safely "inside" us, we can be separate from them for long periods without worry. Some people find it very difficult to let those they love out of their sight. When the beloved is not available, they become anxious and frightened. Such people are called possessive or jealous. Jealousy is the fear of losing someone we love, and it goes back to the child's fear of losing its key attachment figure. However, most people find a balance between closeness and separateness, and this reflects the reliable presence of parental figures in the early years of life.

The growing autonomy of the child leads to independent activity. It wants to explore its surroundings; it sometimes touches and amuses itself with things it should not. These are moments that lead to frustration, which is associated with anger. Anger and love are closely linked. They are the opposite sides of the same coin. Some psychologists locate the roots of frustration and anger in the first few months of life, but it is usually in the second and third year, the time of the beginning of autonomy, when anger is seen most clearly. The child wants to do or handle things its own way, but a parent says "no," and there is conflict. If the child persists, the parent shouts or even smacks, and temporarily there is a rupture of the relationship. After a few seconds or moments, there is reconciliation, forgiveness, and reparation.

As adults we also say and do things that hurt those we love, and then we feel guilty. After a while we forgive, or

are forgiven, we make amends, and the relationship is restored.

In adult relationships we encounter people who do
not negotiate conflict this smoothly. When they hurt
someone, they cannot accept responsibility for their behavior. They blame everyone else. Some people find it
impossible to apologize. When they have done something wrong, they withdraw into themselves and refuse
to be reached. This is called sulking, and some men and
women will sulk for hours, even days. In such instances
reconciliation is hard to achieve.

How Self-Esteem Grows

Slowly the growing child is building its self-esteem,
that is, love of itself. Self-esteem is realized through the
child feeling that its sensations, actions, thoughts, and
feelings are good. This leads to basic self-acceptance.
Through this self-acceptance, it trusts itself and feels lovable.

Self-esteem is based on the constant affirmation the
child receives from its parents and others. Through them
it feels that it is good. This goodness is transmitted unconditionally simply on the basis that the child is present
and exists. It does not have to do anything to merit this
approval. It is simply lovable because it is there. The way
it experiences this lovability is by feeling recognized,
wanted, and appreciated.

Self-esteem plays a vital role in human relationships. If
we feel lovable, then we allow people to get close to us
and love us. We are not afraid of what they will discover
when they approach us. We have nothing to hide. People
who have a lot of self-esteem have a basic goodness at
the center of their personality. They do not need to put
on extra external decoration in appearance or status.
They present themselves as they are and expect to be ap-

preciated as such. Those who are unsure of themselves seek to boost their self-esteem by additional embellishment. Equally those who are full of self-esteem feel they have something of value to offer to others. Their most precious gift is their self, and they do not hesitate to donate themselves fully.

At about the age of five, children go to school, having mastered the abilities of separation from parents, a certain independence, command of language, the ability to take initiatives, play on their own, and, up to a point, become self-reliant. They are ready to acquire the three Rs. Now cognitive training begins in earnest.

Until this time their self-esteem, the feeling of being lovable, has grown through parental nurturing, that is, on the child's ability to experience feelings of being recognized, wanted, and appreciated. During the school years, self-esteem will be built on the results of industry and achievement. School, with its marks, reports, and examinations, offers a visible indication of success or failure.

Self-esteem can now be built both from feeling loved by parents and through the results of schoolwork. This dual basis of self-esteem, coming both from home and school, has important implications for adult love. If the child does not acquire the feeling of unconditional love on the basis of being a person in his or her own right, love and approval become solely dependent on achievement. The consequence of this is that in adult relationships there is no expectation to be loved for one's own sake. Every bit of approval has to be earned through performance. The husband or the wife who have been brought up in this way expect only to be appreciated when they fulfill their roles at home and work. Their understanding of love is based on achievement, and they can enjoy approval only when they feel they have earned it. Their whole life of love is based on a routine contract.

They expect to discharge their responsibilities to the full and be praised or criticized accordingly. They can be extremely critical of themselves and of their spouse if they fail to deliver the appropriate and required behavior.

Between the ages of seven and ten, children reach a point of development when they no longer accept the authority of parents and teachers unconditionally. They begin to argue back, to question absolute authority, expect justifying reasons for rules and regulations, and feel treated unfairly when parents and teachers use their authority without adequate reason. These are the years when homes and classrooms reverberate with the words, "It's not fair."

The feeling of being asked to do something that violates their integrity, or feeling exploited in any way, forms a deep groove in the emerging personality, and the whole sense of justice is linked with it. They expect to have their rights respected, to be treated fairly. They expect their integrity to be safeguarded by everyone, but particularly by those who claim to love them. This is why they feel particularly hurt when they are let down by those close to them, who, in failing them, elicit their deepest anger.

The Effects of Puberty

The beginning of the second decade is the time when puberty commences. Secondary sexual characteristics emerge in both females and males. Nature has now prepared boys and girls to be physically attracted to each other, and to be mutually drawn to one another ultimately for the sake of sexual intercourse.

This is the time when the separation between children and parents takes a further decisive step. Puberty is also the time of overt prohibition of incestuous relationships. Sadly these boundaries are sometimes broken by fathers and stepfathers, and sexual abuse occurs at puberty, or even before.

After the arrival of puberty, adolescence follows, lasting until the early twenties. Adolescence is a time when the final stage of autonomy takes place. Young people separate from their parents, find independent work, or continue with higher studies. They begin to be interested in sexual relationships.

This is the time when courtships begin, and adolescents begin a series of emotional and sexual encounters until they find someone with whom they fall in love. Sometimes they fall in love with more than one person, until someone emerges as the chosen one, and marriage or cohabitation begins.

Most men and women want to experience love from each other through marriage. Thus marriage becomes the second intimate relationship of love in life, and yet, instead of finding love, many couples break up and their marriages end in divorce. There are many reasons for divorce, but some of them are established in the course of the first intimate relationship of love in childhood when some people are hurt or wounded. These are emotional wounds that they carry into marriage, and there, in the intimacy of this second loving relationship, they re-live the difficulties, frustrations, and anger of their childhood experiences.

It is vital, therefore, to look at some of these common hurts and wounds in the next chapter.

4

Childhood Hurts and Wounds

A normal childhood should give us the feeling that we are lovable and good, that is, we can emerge in adult life with sufficient self-esteem to feel recognized, wanted, and appreciated simply because we exist. Of course this experience does not excuse us from the task of working and further developing our potential, but everyone who has received unconditional love in childhood feels at least some of the above lovability. At the other end of the spectrum, we may feel unlovable, have low self-esteem, and be hungry for affection. In general, there are small minorities at either end of the spectrum, with most people somewhere in the middle.

When we lean toward the negative side, we have difficulty persuading ourselves that anyone wants or appreciates us. We are constantly surprised when people find us attractive or want our company. We feel shy and lack confidence, and are extremely grateful for the slightest notice given to us. We expect criticism, but when we receive it we are doubly hurt because we have no reserve of good feelings to cushion it. We may get excessively angry at trivial upsets, shout and scream, or we may suppress our anger and feel depressed.

As hurt people, we are delighted when we are befriended, but expect to be abandoned very easily. When we are receiving love, we feel that at long last our needs are being met, only to discover that we find it very difficult to believe, and sometimes even push away those who love us. Or, we sometimes test them continuously to ensure that they are genuine.

When these points are explained to men and women who have difficulties with relationships, they are astonished. Some of them realize their childhood was not ideal, but they still felt "loved" by their parents. Others think it is their own fault, their parents gave them everything and it is they who made a mess of things.

In practice, of course, it is not always the parents' fault. In any case, fault is the wrong word. Perhaps as parents these people offered their children the best that was available at the time. But parents are not the only contributors to love. Genes play a part. Our capacity to receive love depends on our make-up, too, and some people can receive affirmation much more easily than others. Thus, the love we feel as adults can be a mixture of the parenting we received and our genetic inheritance.

Nevertheless, many are still surprised when they are faced with the possibility that their parents were not as loving as they thought they were. When they begin to examine the matter in detail, they may find that, while their parents took care of them physically and educationally, in other words fed and clothed them, provided them with adequate material benefits and sent them to good schools, they actually did not feel close to one or both parents.

The parents may have found it difficult to demonstrate affection, and may have rarely picked up, hugged, or caressed their children. Feelings may rarely have been displayed. Both parents may have worked and had little time for children. Criticism may have been rampant, and appreciation or approval scarce. Such children may have felt ignored for long periods, and were only noticed when they broke some rule.

Most people can recognize overt physical abuse, but it's hard to recognize emotional neglect. Yet many childhood wounds are inflicted by the absence of affection and affirmation in subtle ways, which happens, for example, when parents prefer one sibling over another. Whatever the reason, there are many people who emerge from childhood without the experience of unconditional love, and this becomes a handicap when they are expecting to be loved, or when they try to love others.

The Disorders of Attachment

As we have already seen, the capacity to form a bond is fundamental to loving. There are people who find it difficult to form an attachment. For example, young people who suffer from autism or adults with schizophrenic illnesses find it difficult to form relationships. Those who sufficiently overcome their problems and form an attachment live with the constant fear of losing their loved ones or being abandoned by them. They form what is known as "anxious attachments."

Jealousy and possessiveness are by-products of these anxious attachments. Such men and women constantly feel threatened in their relationships. They imagine their spouse having affairs when they are doing nothing of the

sort, and they are overwhelmed with panic and despera-
tion when they are. They expect to be supplanted with
extraordinary ease, and all that the husband or wife has
to do is to look at another woman or man, and there is
hell to pay. Often such people are not only anxious about
being abandoned, but they also live with the dread that
something terrible will happen to their loved ones, so
that if a spouse is little late in coming home, for example,
they are overwhelmed with forebodings of tragedy.

Given this anxiety, they long to be physically close to
their spouse, and when this is not possible, to be in telephone contact. Their hunger for physical closeness makes
them possessive, for they dread to let their spouse out of
sight. Their partner feels like a prisoner, and finds it very
difficult to be or do things alone. The need for the physical presence of another person is a normal requirement
of companionship and is part of loving. However, the
possessive hunger for the presence of the spouse is an expression of excessive anxiety. Very often such an anxious
person simply wants the spouse to be physically present.

A second disordered attachment is the "avoidant" one.
Here the spouse finds it very difficult to tolerate closeness of any description. They want to be left alone, and
they remain aloof. They are busy with their own concerns, and they are often undemonstrative. They appear
cold and uninterested and like to keep their distance.
Such an avoidant person is in real difficulty, especially
when they are married to an anxious person who needs a
great deal of closeness. However, being avoidant is problematic even for "normal" personalities.

The Disorders of Trust
Trust is fundamental to all human relationships, but
particularly to people who are in an intimate loving exchange. In fact, trust is essential for survival. We need to

feel that we will not be hurt by those to whom we entrust ourselves completely. Hence all physical and emotional violence is a violation of trust. Since loving intimacy expects sexual intercourse, trust is essential at the moment we abandon all our defenses and become united in coitus.

Emotionally, trust is the foundation of the continuity of our loving relationship with another human being. If physical trust is the basis of our safety, emotional trust is essential for the hope that we will continue to be loved. Emotional trust may be strong or weak. People with weak trust are suspicious, cynical, and expect very little from life. They emerge from a childhood in which they had little reason to feel that anyone was reliable or trustworthy. Their parents did not keep promises, were inconsistent, and perhaps even told lies. They grew up expecting to be let down, and consider everyone a potential source of further hurt.

This hurt is experienced particularly from those who are close to us when they fail to recognize, appreciate, or make us feel wanted. The possible range of feeling let down is infinite, but it shows particularly when the spouse has an affair. That is when trust vanishes. Regaining trust after experiencing infidelity may be very difficult, and it may never return to the previous levels.

Trust is also essential in communication. If normal life is to continue, we must believe in those who relate to us, particularly those who claim to love us. If they tell us lies, half truths, or hide essentials from us, the foundations are laid for distrust which is corrosive to a loving relationship. Very often we tell lies because we are afraid that we will hurt the person we love or that they will be angry with us. When lie follows lie, the situation becomes unsustainable, and the final position is much worse than if we told the truth and faced the consequences.

The Disorders of Autonomy

Autonomy is linked with our freedom and independence. When we commit ourselves to love another person, we are at the same time reducing our freedom to form an exclusive relationship with someone else and accepting the responsibility of faithfulness. Furthermore, central to loving is offering our availability. We offer our body, mind, and feelings to the one to whom we make our exclusive commitment. These restrictions are self-imposed and are usually accepted as the necessary conditions for the unique loving intimacy of marriage.

But we may have problems in this area. We may have had parents who were domineering, possessive, exacting, demanding, overbearing, and our freedom and independence may have become extra-precious in our life. We may want the advantages of intimacy, but resent the restrictions on our freedom and independence. So, particularly in the early years of marriage, we enjoy sex, caring, and affection, but we want to go on as if we were single and use our time the way we want. We go home for food and sex, and use the rest of the time to work, play, and amuse ourselves with our friends. We have no time to meet the needs of our spouse. When she is critical, we become angry. When he requests something, we interpret it as a demand. Such people treat their spouses as restricting and demanding parents, against whom they angrily rebel.

Every satisfactory loving relationship has to work out a balance between availability and independence, dependence and autonomy, closeness and separation. On the one hand, couples can be so close and dependent on each other that they are described as "fused." Such spouses cannot do anything independently, and they rely entirely on each other. Each loves "with the permission of the other," feeling that they are incomplete without each other.

On the other hand, couples can be so independent that they hardly come near each other. Extremely independent relationships are the basis for so called "open" marriages, in which the partners agree to have extramarital relationships without the spouse minding. The trouble with such arrangements is that sooner or later one spouse begins to feel jealous. Furthermore, while such arrangements are undertaken in the name of freedom, they are usually a mutual expression of the inability to accept limitations.

The Disorders of Accomplishment

The point has been made already that self-esteem is built on the unconditional love given to us by our parents. When children lack the feeling of being loved on the basis of their intrinsic worth, they fall back on the conditional love that they can earn through their accomplishments. In adult life, such people enter relationships based on give and take. Because they don't feel wanted for their own sake, they do things for others on a contractual basis. In effect, they say to their spouse, "I will do this for you, if you do that for me."

When for some reason such men or women are not in a position to be productive, they lose their self-esteem completely. If, for example, they become unemployed, they don't feel any worth, and there is good evidence that marital breakdown is often related to unemployment. An alternative distortion is the person who works excessively as the whole basis for finding value, and takes no pleasure in doing anything together with the partner or spending time with the children.

The Disorders of Dependence

The whole of childhood is a gradual separation from parental figures and those in authority. It is a covenant of gradual independence, in which the growing person learns to decide, cope, handle fear, plan, anticipate, and overcome threats to survival. They emerge as autonomous, self-reliant, self-governing, and self-directing.

Some people achieve physical and intellectual maturity without an equivalent emotional one. They look and behave as adults, but feel unsure, uncertain, frightened, and still feel they need to rely on somebody stronger than themselves.

Marriages between such an emotionally dependent person and someone who appears strong, dominant, and assertive are common. Dependent people can be either sex, and they marry for security in the widest sense of that word.

With the passage of time, such dependent people grow up and realize their emotional potential. They no longer need their partner to make decisions for them, where to go, what to do, to make up their minds, to shape their opinions, and set their values. They no longer idealize or magnify the importance of their spouse. They can make an equivalent contribution to the relationship. This is a good outcome, but there are alternative and dangerous ones.

The most common problem with such a relationship is that the dependent spouse will outgrow the parental partner. When they have attained their confidence, they will no longer need the security of their spouse. They no longer need the "permission" of another for their decisions. These are the men and women who claim they are no longer in love with their partner. Their "love" was linked to their dependence. When the dependence disappears, so does the love, and the marriage comes to an end.

Another problem is that the so-called "strong" person is in fact assertive, driving, domineering, but behind this strength there may be an equally needy and emotionally deprived person. There comes a time when the dominant partner expresses underlying needs and yearns for support, affection, and understanding. These moments may come when the dominant person is sick, tired, under pressure, or when things go wrong, like losing a parent, a friend, or a job. He or she sends out a signal for help, but the partner neither recognizes it, nor is capable of helping. Dominant persons are only acceptable as long as they have no needs. If they do show their needy side, their dependent partner, who usually feels they have nothing to offer, is overwhelmed and may run away.

Though many people operate out of one or more of these disorders, the majority of people are not seriously wounded by them. They proceed to their adolescence forming relationships and sooner or later fall in love with a particular man or woman. In the next chapter I will describe this state of falling in love as it happens for most of us.

5

Falling in Love

During adolescence, a number of social and psychological situations occur that prepare young people to fall
in love. They have separated from their parents, that is,
they experience aloneness. This aloneness sensitizes them
to the need for togetherness. Beyond togetherness, men
and women long for an independent abode in which they
can organize and control their lives. They want a home
of their own. Cohabitation or marriage, particularly the
latter, is a sign of adulthood. Through marriage, they can
assume adult roles. Society is organized around married
adults, a state to which most people aspire.

Thus through aloneness, the desire for a home of
one's own, and the authority and status that marriage
confer, most people are propelled toward coupling.

Before they reach this stage, however, they date a variety of people. They form transitory relationships and find out whether they like the person they are with. They go out to eat, to the movies, concerts or outings, and they experiment with interacting. They assess whether they find each other sufficiently physically attractive, share the same ideas and outlook on life, want the same things, and are comfortable with each other. There is excitement in discovering these things.

Ultimately someone is preferred and becomes special. At this stage, two people fall in love with each other. Millions of words have been written to describe the state of being in love. It is a state of intense longing for union with another. Reciprocal love (union with the other) is associated with fulfillment and ecstasy, unrequited love with emptiness, anxiety, or despair. There are several essential aspects of falling in love.

At the heart of it is physical attraction. Both sexes are highly attracted by each other's bodies. Although there is some agreement about physical beauty, there is no way that the special attraction of another's physical appearance can be defined. Attraction is based on a whole variety of factors, but it should be noted that vision, finding the other pleasing to the eyes; sound, being attracted by their voice; and touch, enjoying being held and stroked, are all essential. Physical excitation is thus stimulated by the same elements as those which form the attachment between ourselves and our mother. Falling in love is a resuscitation of the physical and emotional links that form our primary emotional attachment to mother, and it is a repeat in adult life of our infantile bonds.

But in addition to the gratification of vision, sound, and touch, there is now an overall sexual dimension. Women and men now convey erotic excitation, and men long to touch the breasts and buttocks of women.

Women are stimulated by general appearance of strength and the contours of the male body. Both sexes, but particularly men, are erotically aroused through touch, kissing, and physical closeness, ultimately wanting sexual intercourse. The physical passion is intense.

Emotionally, couples need to be exclusively special to each other, to feel recognized, wanted, and appreciated. The person they fall in love with makes them aware that they matter, that they are special. They feel needed and there is a mutuality of significance. When they are together, everyone else fades into insignificance. Nobody else exists who is remotely comparable in importance, and the loved one occupies the center of thoughts all the time. This occupation is intrusive since thoughts of the beloved person cannot easily be put aside.

Beyond physical and emotional attraction, there is social fitness. We are usually attracted by people who are of the same intelligence and interests and who share our values and opinions. A number of problems arise when we find we are attracted physically to someone who does not share our interests or is not of the same background as ourselves. The conflict is between the heart and the head.

Thus we are usually attracted by someone we like physically, emotionally, and socially. Once we have fallen in love, we are in a state of emotional excitement, in some form of ecstasy, and several things happen in that state.

We tend to idealize the person we love. By idealization is meant that we tend to think of our beloved as the most attractive, desirable, and suitable person in the world. We are not in a mood to find fault with him or her. If we detect shortcomings, we reduce their importance. If the beloved upsets us, we tend to forgive and forget quickly. We want to believe that there is nothing wrong with the one we love.

The state of idealized excitement elicits a marked desire for closeness and contact. We spend hours on the telephone, write pages and pages of letters, and spend every possible moment with each other. There is an enormous longing for closeness and especially for sexual intercourse.

This is the positive, ecstatic side of being in love. There is also, however, a negative, painful, and depressive side. When the loved one is silent, withdrawn, or is reluctant to be as close as we want them to be, we fear that they are no longer interested in us and this causes deep distress. One moment is full of excitement and the next heralds despair.

When the telephone rings or the letter arrives, there is a great deal of excitement. The passionate response can actually involve the body: The heart beats faster, the muscles get tense, and the face gets flushed. There is a state of profound physiological arousal. The body trembles with excitement at the anticipation of even momentary closeness. Thoughts cannot be controlled because they are obsessed with the beloved. Concentration on work becomes difficult because of preoccupation with the beloved.

In the presence of such intensity of love, the fear of losing the loved one is very real. Hence there are moments of intense jealousy when he or she looks at someone else or even temporarily abandons the relationship for another person. The scorn that is poured on the intruder is immense because it is difficult to conceptualize anyone more attractive than oneself.

To sum up, romantic love is one of the most powerful activators of our pleasure centers, and tends to be very exciting emotionally. Being with the person, or even just thinking of them, is highly stimulating. Being in love is, by definition, the strongest positive feeling we can have.

Other things, stimulant drugs, passionate causes, manic states, can induce powerful changes in our brains, but none so reliably, so enduringly, or so delightfully, as that "right" other person. If the relationship is not established securely or is uncertain, anxiety or other displeasure centers may be active as well, producing a situation of great emotional turmoil as the lover swings between hope and torment.

Being in love is not a state that lasts forever. Couples decide to bring the agony of separation to a close and live together in the form of cohabitation, usually marriage. While the ardor of feelings may last for years for some couples, the intensity usually wanes and the couple enter a period of "loving" which may last up to fifty years or more.

When it comes to loving, we know very little of its components. What is it that keeps a couple together for such a long time? In the next three chapters, I will describe what I consider three essential components of loving, based on observation and clinical experience.

6

Sustaining Love

There is widespread evidence that the ecstasy experienced during the stage of falling in love is short-lived. The high state of emotion subsides and the couple have to survive at a different level of maturity. There are four characteristics that I consider essential during this "sustaining" aspect of loving. They are availability, communication, demonstration of affection, and resolution of conflict.

The Characteristic of Availability

I have already mentioned several times that human beings, like the other higher animals, form attachments to one another. These are based on vision, seeing one another, sound, hearing one another, and touching one another's bodies. During the state of being in love, there was an intensification of this togetherness. Togetherness remains a key factor in availability. The fact of seeing, hearing, and touching gives one intense gratification, and so being in the presence of each other remains a regular need for couples.

There are a number of things that operate against this togetherness. Men and women are busy during the day with their work, and when they come home in the evening they are occupied with the children, cooking the evening meal, and cleaning up. By that time it is late, and they want to go to bed. Thus they are not available to each other. In bed one or both may want or need to read, and thus they are still not interacting with each other.

But there are other reasons for not spending time together. The working schedule may be such that the couple leave early in the morning and arrive home late at night. If they manage to come home early, very often they spend the evening entertaining or going out with friends. On the weekends there are things to catch up on, shopping to do, jobs around the house, or office work continued on Saturday and Sunday. Couples who entertain, or are entertained a lot, rarely have private access to one another.

It is imperative that time be allocated for the couple to be with their children and also to be alone with each other. This is the time to be still and be aware of the partner, to simply gaze and take notice of a new dress, hair style, suit, and admire these things. So often spouses ignore these small but important changes in the other's style of life. A moment's recognition gives the feeling that one exists and is important. Both sexes have to guard against being taken for granted. Many women work out of the home today and yet they remain the primary housekeepers. Moments of personal awareness are important to shake the feeling of being used. Couples can be so busy struggling for survival that they have no time for each other.

Another form of availability is the togetherness of accomplishing a shared task. Clearing the table and washing dishes together are probably the most common shared tasks. Decorating the house or gardening can be carried out together. Shopping can be a weekly event for the couple. In all these activities there is the pleasure of being in each other's presence and accomplishing a task. This togetherness also assures that the couple is going to stay together and is planning for a future together.

Though this togetherness is extremely important, couples need to balance it with separateness. This separateness is usually achieved by working at separate jobs. But there are moments on the weekend when one or the other wants to be alone for a while. This has to be respected. The modern term is "giving space" to each other. This space can be occupied by playing a sport, gardening, constructing things, reading, or listening to music. The right balance between closeness and separateness has to be worked out for each couple, and may alter at stages of their life. What is important, however, is that, while the rhythm of this tension is preserved, they are there for one another in times of need.

This takes us to the next experience of availability: developing appropriate empathy. By empathy I mean an awareness of the inner world of the other person, and the ability to respond accurately to the needs of the moment. The awareness is a matter of accurately reading moods. If the mood is one of distress, it is important to ask why the spouse is distressed. Is it the sadness of losing a friend, or hearing that someone they love is ill, or the disappointment of something not achieved, or frustration at something having gone wrong? We have to respond to the apprehensions, anxieties, and fears of our partner, and often it is our availability that relieves their discomfort.

The ability to discern the inner world of our partner depends on our ability to know our spouse well, anticipate their reactions, and read the cues they give us accurately. They may look sad, apprehensive, full of joy, or be shaking with fear. To be read accurately by those who love us is a reminder of our earliest experiences when mother or father knew our inner world instinctively, even before we could speak. We still love to be surprised by the sympathetic and appreciative comments of our partner, without having to ask for them. It gives us a feeling of real closeness and being properly understood. It shows us that our partner is in touch with us and wants to reach us before we call out.

This high degree of empathy is not widely available. Most of the time we need to be informed about what is going on, but we relish the moments when we do react spontaneously.

Being There at Key Moments

Beyond the availability of togetherness, task-orientation, and empathy, there is the presence of the spouse at key moments of our life. When couples recount the accumulation of distressing experiences that have led them to the point of separation, the absence or neglect of their partner at a key moment plays an important role.

Times of illness or experiences of pain are one of these key moments. It should be remembered that when we were very young and acutely dependent on our parents for survival, physical or emotional distress were crucial experiences that made us run to them for help. Throughout childhood and adult life, we are encouraged to cope with illness and distress by being brave and keeping a stiff upper lip.

Yet psychology has taught us that it is better to show our emotions and seek comfort when we need it, without, of course, turning into hypochondriacs. Illness is a time when we not only experience discomfort, but, if serious, our very survival is at stake. At these times we regress to an earlier stage of our life, and we need to be picked up and comforted. Most spouses are in fact likely to respond with sensitivity and care to illness, and look after the other when they are incapacitated, but some do run away from illness. They find it frightening and feel helpless before it. Instead of being supportive and nurturing, they turn their backs and disappear.

Another negative response is to attack the sick person and blame them for their illness on the grounds that they did not take care of themselves. Sometimes the sick person does not want to be fussed over, and they repulse all attention, but normally we become dependent when we are sick, and we look for a facilitating response from our partner.

Illness is closely allied to death. Spouses lose their parents at any time, but they themselves are usually in their forties and fifties when this happens. The illness and death of a parent is another key moment of availability. The sickness that may precede death for months or years is a time when the spouse is stretched to the limit. They need the support of their partner. This support may mean looking after the children while the spouse is away, having the elderly parent at home, visiting the hospital, or actually nursing the sick parent. All this imposes a great deal of strain on a couple. It is a moment of heightened need, and most partners respond generously, but not all. There is the spouse who complains about the absences of their partner who is busy visiting or nursing the elderly parent. They do not want to be left alone or to take care of themselves. They urge their spouse to put their parent in a nursing home, and under no circumstances are they prepared to have the person in their own home. These acts of obstruction are very painful and are interpreted as callous.

At the time of the death of an elderly parent, the bereaved spouse needs time to grieve. That is to say, they need time to cry as a protest against the loss, a reminder of the way the young child protests at its mother's absence. This is followed by searching, as the baby did for its mother, the actual visiting of the grave if buried, and finally, the long period of detachment as they get accustomed to the loss.

At the other end of the spectrum, there are moments of creativity and joy. This begins with the delivery of a newborn. While labor has painful moments, in general giving birth is an exciting and happy experience for both spouses. The mother wants to share it with her husband. Nowadays this is possible in the majority of circumstances. There is no excuse for the husband to be missing. Most husbands do not, of course, miss the occasion, but some do. They are not in the country, are traveling, or much worse, they are found drunk in a bar celebrating with their friends. The absence of the father from the birth of the child is something most wives never forget, and is often brought up later when adverse complications occur in the relationship.

Another joyous event (for some!) is a birthday. It is a special moment, and it means a lot when it is remembered. It shows that a special time in the life of the spouse is recollected and commemorated. The same is true of anniversaries. The day calls for a celebration. When overlooked, it is not only that the day is forgotten, but that the spouse has been ignored. Finally, holidays are a special time. They can be a time of renewal for the couple who combine all the factors of availability, the togetherness, doing things, a high degree of empathy about what pleases each other, and time to realize it. Sadly, holidays can be spoiled by arguing about activities and worrying about expenses.

Availability is the key to loving in that its various forms remind the couple of the presence of mother or father in childhood, coupled with the safety and security that togetherness presented them. It is the principal feature of exclusivity, and it brings about the daily unity of the couple. When it is freely present, spouses can bask in the knowledge that they exist for each other, and the strength that this gives makes them available to their children and to others. When it is present, it is often taken for granted, but it causes acute distress when it is missing.

The Characteristic of Communication

The next characteristic for sustaining love is verbal communication. There are major differences between men and women when it comes to communication. Women are often much better at it. In fact, when men find it hard to communicate and can't cope with women who do, they call it nagging! There are other differences as well. Men tend to intellectualize, while women tend to be concerned with feelings and intuition. This does not mean for one moment that women are not capable of reason, or men of feelings and intuition. Yet these contrasting approaches often lead to extended arguments. Such encounters between the sexes can be creative and produce rich results. At their worst, when the complementarity is not appreciated, couples argue and disagree, calling each other wrong. They are not wrong; they are simply expressing different facets of the truth.

Another aspect of communication is the ability of the listener to make sense of what the other is saying, especially when the verbalizing spouse is upset or confused. The partner who is listening can discern patterns of meaning which the speaker cannot. This discerning depends on the ability to listen carefully to the partner. Sometimes we are so anxious to have our say that we are not paying attention to what our spouse is saying. We simply want them to stop talking so that we can start. When we do listen, we should do so non-judgmentally. We should not make judgmental remarks or pepper our responses with criticism. Rather we should affirm the spouse. We are very good at affirming children, but we forget that adults need praise as well. It is only too easy to forget to give thanks for meals cooked, for a clean house, the care of the children, the sweat of work, and many other daily routines.

Communication needs to be clear, shared, non-judgmental, appreciative, and informative. This is an essential part of loving and is a grave handicap when not present. And, of course, communication can have a negative side, especially if spouses shower abuse on each other. By the time that point is reached, the relationship is in bad shape and needs counseling.

Demonstrating Affection

Couples need to experience recurrent demonstrations of affection from each other, apart from having sexual intercourse. I have often counseled couples who say, "He or she never says I love you," and the spouse replies, "I told you I loved you twenty-five years ago. Why do you need to hear it again? I'm still here, aren't I?" But feelings are not confined to being there or even to communication. A kiss, a hug, a touch are important moments in which a couple shares intimacy. Spouses want to be told that they love one another. The demonstration of affection is distinctive of the couple who are in touch with each other's inner worlds. In this way they are showing each other that they remain special.

Men are often embarrassed by demonstrations of affection, feeling that they are unmanly, while women cherish such moments as signals of special awareness. Many women complain that men never show affection unless they want sex. In fact some wives know that sex is wanted because they get special attention on that day. Some men express affection by buying things for their wives or doing suitable actions. The trouble is that most wives do not want to be bought. They want to be cherished with words and/or actions.

Being held in the arms of one's spouse is a reminder of the way we were held in the arms of our parents. In our childhood we experienced this cherishing, and it was reinforced by being hugged and kissed. Puberty brought a level of eroticism to the same behavior, but affection remained the infrastructure. Recurrent expressions of affection remain a constant need for couples, just as for children. Though such warm, affectionate exchange can often be the prelude to sexual intercourse, it has validity and value of its own.

Resolving Conflict

When a couple live in the modern atmosphere of egalitarian relationships there is bound to be conflict when they disagree, hurt, or are aggressive toward each other. Under these circumstances, there is often a victor and a vanquished. Either partner can win an argument and feel vindicated, but, at the heart of a loving relationship, the goal of conflict is not victory or defeat but getting closer to each other. When we feel angry it is because we have not been heard or have been misunderstood, and we feel rejected, ignored, or let down. We may shout and scream or show our upset quietly. The whole point of such expressions of anger is not to win an argument, but to register a point of view. Our anger is mobilized because we have been hurt, and a constructive quarrel is one in which the partner recognizes the pain we have experienced. The anger should be a signal for us to avoid the distress we have caused. Ideally, as our moments of anger are understood, the occasions for outbursts will decrease in frequency. When quarreling escalates, there is a fundamental problem in the relationship and help should be sought.

A constructive argument, usually followed by forgiveness and resolution of tension, should also lead to discovering the vulnerability of our partner so we can make efforts toward helping them overcome their difficulty. Constructive arguments should also help us avoid repeating the pattern of behavior that incites controversy. In the latter case, our aim should also be to help our partner overcome difficulties. This leads us to the second aspect of loving, which is our attempt to heal our spouse, that is, to provide him or her with the means of overcoming difficulties, and that is the subject of the next chapter.

7

Healing Love

Many people emerge from childhood wounded, and they have great difficulty experiencing intimacy. To a greater or lesser extent, we are all wounded people, but some more so than others.

In the last hundred years, psychoanalysis has taught us that there are ways of responding to hurt people that give them a chance for healing. A few people obtain these chances through psychoanalysis and psychotherapy. At the heart of psychoanalysis are two models of change. The first and classic one is transference. In this reaction, the patient experiences the analyst as a parental figure and re-lives through him or her earlier childhood experiences that are interpreted by the therapist. Thus the patient can learn new ways of feeling that are more appropriate for effective functioning as an adult. The second model depends partially on this exchange, but even more on learning from the therapist a more effective way of being.

Very few people can afford to undergo analysis or therapy, but most human beings do enter the depths of intimacy through marriage. There they can experience their spouse as a parental figure, and provided the right interaction takes place, there is a second chance of learning at this level about relationships. This is one basis of healing. There are two other forms of healing currently practiced in psychology. The first is behavior therapy. There are many aspects to this therapy, but basically behavior is shaped by rewards and punishments. This is, in fact, how most of us relate to one another. When we are pleased with what we experience, we reward the person, and in this way encourage the repetition of the particular conduct. The reward can take any form in marriage, from praise to sexual intercourse, whatever pleases the partner. When the behavior is unpleasant or painful, we respond in a punitive manner. In marriage, spouses withdraw from each other, and either withhold behavior that pleases or actually deliver something unpleasant. In ordinary life, the behavioristic model is the one that operates most commonly. We are pleased when things go well and angry when they do not.

There is a third model based on cognitive therapy. In this approach, we appeal to the learning mechanism of another person to help them see that what they are experiencing, saying, or doing is wrong, and we offer alternative ways of seeing things. This is an attempt to change people by appealing to their understanding of life.

Spouses can work in all three ways with their partners. First of all they can try to understand how they are experienced as parental figures. Women seem to find it easi-

er to see themselves in the role of mother and their husbands as the child, despite manly appearance and conduct. Husbands find it more difficult to see themselves as
fathers, with their wives in the role of little girls, but
there is no doubt that both partners can continue in the
parental role. It is important to assess the parental role
that one has been put in, and to make efforts to help the
spouse act independently. In other words, one should let
the partner be responsible for his or her own life, making
their own decisions, or making up their own minds, and
doing for themselves the things they find difficult.

The second thing each partner should recognize is the
defenses that their spouse has developed. Dynamic psychology has shown that each of us creates a distinctive
way of protecting ourselves psychologically from anxiety
and pain. Initially Freud concentrated on the defenses to
which we resort to guard ourselves from unacceptable aggression and sexuality; but we build up defenses to cover
up a wide range of painful experiences. We use the mechanisms of denial, projection, and rationalization, among
others which are unconscious, to avoid facing painful re-
alities. We deny responsibility for our actions. We deny
our fears, aggressive feelings, and our lust. We say that it
is not for us, but our partner who is entertaining these
ideas, or we offer some trite explanation for our conduct.

It is vital in healing to recognize what defense our
spouse is using. Handling his or her repetitive defenses is
a special task of healing. The mistake we make is to resort
to moralistic language. When a partner repeatedly denies
the damaging actions they perform, we call this failure to
own up lying. When they offer an explanation of why
they cannot do something we have asked them to do, we
call them lazy. When they put their interest before ours,
we call them selfish, instead of finding out why they find
it difficult to be generous.

The homes of millions of couples reverberate with this moralistic language, which is tossed to and fro as a form of abuse: "Oh, my spouse is lazy, selfish, self-centered, and a liar, too." These accusations are constantly present in counseling sessions. What is needed is patience to discover why the spouse is behaving in this particular way, using a particular defense, and gently confront him or her with reality. If spouses are accused in moral terms, they simply dig their heels in, further protecting their character. The debate shifts from finding what is really wrong to mutually protecting their self-esteem from each other's attacks.

Avoid Moralistic Language

An essential part of healing is to avoid using moralistic language and to persist in confronting the partner with their defenses. When this has been achieved, help is given to overcome the particular difficulty. These difficulties are associated with anxiety, fear, lack of initiative, and self-esteem. In general, their fear is that they cannot cope with something in life, and so they avoid it or take an easier route. For example, the husband says he had no time to carry out his wife's request, when, in fact, he forgot because he has a poor memory to which he cannot own up. Or, the wife makes the husband call the garage or a builder to argue over the bill because she cannot face arguments.

Another difficulty many have is saying no to requests they get, for fear of upsetting the person who has asked the favor. All of us have many small or big difficulties for which we make excuses. The trouble is, we are compliant with strangers. With them we never lose our temper, but we go home and let loose an almighty rage. This is the defense of displacement. We usually displace our anger from those we fear to those with whom we are familiar.

Thus wives can complain of husbands who will do any-thing for a neighbor, but never put up a shelf in their own home—all because they cannot say no. While the wife is sweet to all her friends, she may be frustrated and angry at home where everything irritates her. These are typical examples of displacement.

Couples are indeed loving each other when they rec-ognize the parental role they are being put in and refuse to accept it, or do so for a while with their eyes open to what they are doing. They can then recognize the specif-ic defense their spouse uses, understand what anxiety, fear, anger is being hidden, and confront that reality in-stead of bombarding the partner with moralistic lan-guage, a form of destructive abuse.

If couples can do these two things consistently from the beginning of their relationship, the way to healing has begun.

When the confrontation with the fear, anxiety, or an-ger is made, the next step is not to humiliate the spouse for having such a trait. It is not considered a weakness, nor is a judgmental approach made. The anxiety is rec-ognized and the spouse is encouraged to face and over-come it. This will not take place at once. The diffident person will not suddenly summon the courage to be an-gry or say no to requests, but a start can be made, and every time a success is scored, it is rewarded so that the new learning takes root in the personality.

In this way some of the most common anxieties, such as lack of confidence and low self-esteem, can be over-come when the spouse is systematically encouraged to give up avoidance techniques, such as not taking on chal-lenges or apologizing needlessly for one's existence. At the heart of these two problems is the feeling that one is not lovable or worthwhile.

Everyone is worthwhile, and the spouse can give his

wife or her husband a feeling of unconditional acceptance, and slowly encourage them to believe in themselves. Healing in these instances is a matter of giving nurture and succor to someone who needs it, and at the same time encouraging them to undertake new challenges with the confidence that they will succeed.

This healing is relatively easy when one spouse is wounded and the other is more stable and mature and has a loving disposition. It becomes more difficult when both parties are wounded people. Even so, their wounds are not likely to be similar, and they can give each other support where they need it most.

After this general introduction about moving from moralizing and guilt-producing attacks to understanding the anxiety that determines behavior, let's move to some specific problems.

The Disorders of Attachment

I have mentioned that about twenty-five percent of people form anxious attachments, and that about the same number are the avoidant form. Let us look at both these problems.

People with anxious attachments are constantly afraid of losing the person they are close to. Such a person tends to cling to their mate, be jealous and possessive, and fearful that they will lose the partner to someone else. Short of losing them, they are apprehensive about them being injured or falling ill.

The response to the person with the anxious attachment is initially to ensure that they are not made unduly anxious. If they are terrified of losing the partner to another man or woman, the partner should try to be as reliable and punctual as possible, to help the spouse feel secure.

But there are limits that should be set to this anxious

behavior. If the anxious partner is restrictive and possessive, that is, attempts to stop the partner from ever going out and having friends or activities outside the home,
this should not be tolerated. Every care should be taken
to encourage the anxious person to overcome their fear
by spending periods away from home, allowing the partner to do likewise, and undertaking independent activities.

A basic anxiety of such a person is the fear of dis-
integration that will ensue if they are left alone. In order
to overcome this fear, they should be encouraged to be
less dependent on the partner and learn to cope and fend
for themselves. The person with anxious attachment has
to gain an inward sense of confidence in their capacity to
survive by themselves. This means stretching their potential while the spouse is alive and available. The spouse
should avoid ridiculing this fear of loss and encourage
self-reliance in every possible way.

The "avoidant" attachment is held by someone whose
anxiety is not about loss but about closeness. They are
afraid of intimacy, which feels to them like an intrusion.
They keep their distance, avoid emotional contact, are re-
served, and do not let people get close to them.
Closeness is very threatening and they remain aloof.

Such people are not easy to know. They are genuinely
afraid of closeness and they do not want to be touched or
to become emotionally involved. They are often criticized for being "stuck up." In fact, behind this veil of
aloofness, they may be yearning for companionship.

The response to such persons is to try to reach them as
far as they will allow it. After that, every effort should be
made to overcome their resistance by making emotional
contact rewarding. Their partner can encourage short periods of physical closeness, touch, kissing, hugging, first
in private and then gradually in public. The whole point
about the avoidant personality is that he or she has to

learn how to experience physical intimacy safely.

Spouses married to an avoidant personality complain that they are cold and distant and that the only time they get close is when they want sex. One way of helping them overcome their difficulty is by encouraging them to be physically close before sex so that they can conquer their hesitation about intimacy.

Disorders of Trust

Some men and women grow up with a very low level of trust. Such people are suspicious, mistrustful, and afraid that they will be let down. At times they become paranoid, that is, they believe that others have malevolent intentions toward them. When these suspicions become set beliefs, not open to reason, they become "delusions" and are held tenaciously.

When anxious attachment is coupled with mistrust, a psychiatric syndrome of morbid jealousy develops, in which the spouse is absolutely convinced that their partner is having an affair with someone, even if there is no evidence to support such a view. Morbid jealousy is rare, but it plays havoc with a marriage relationship. Spouses can be so convinced of their suspicions that they hire private detectives to follow their husband or wife. They examine clothes for evidence of perfume, hairs, or lipstick, and they trace the spouse's moves with incredible detail, convinced that they are having secret assignations. Morbid jealousy is not based on reason, because it is a delusion. Nevertheless, the spouse who is accused should do everything possible to reassure the other, spend as much time with them as possible, and, of course, avoid any incriminating behavior. The important thing is that the partner who is accused needs to understand the nature of the problem, otherwise they become convinced that they are the one going crazy.

The mistrustful person does not extend suspicions to a morbid degree, but they tend to be secretive and guarded. They will keep their papers locked up, and they will hide the things that matter to them from the partner. They are reluctant to disclose their inner world in case the information they reveal is used against them. Such people are described as keeping their cards close to the vest.

Mistrustful people are not easy to reach. They need to be reassured that their confidence will not be betrayed. At the same time, they have to be confronted about their anxieties. Basically they are afraid that if they reveal their inner world, its contents will not be respected, and even worse, will be exploited. These fears have to be challenged. Such people need to discern who they can trust and who may let them down. In building up trust, the spouses have to be careful not to promise beyond their capacity, so they do not let their partner down and reinforce their fears.

Building trust is a slow process, but it enlarges the horizons of both spouses as they reveal more and more of themselves to each other and offers the certainty that their confidences will be respected.

Disorders of Autonomy

Disorders of autonomy often occur in men or women who grew up in homes dominated by one or both parents. For years they had to submit their will to parental wishes, either out of fear or the threat of being kicked out. They grew up resenting authority, and they now refuse to take orders from anybody. The trouble with such a spouse is that the simplest request is interpreted as a demand. They cannot distinguish between natural and normal requirements and unreasonable and authoritarian demands.

Clearly such persons are extremely sensitive to any

approach made to them. The tone of the request is vital, and their cooperation should first be sought before anything is asked of them. A request can be preceded by a clear indication that it is not a demand. An understanding should be reached that distinguishes the spouse from the parent figure, and encourages requests to be considered on their own merit. This is achieved more quickly if the spouse handles the sensitive partner with respect, listens to opinions, pays attention to them, and treats them as responsible adults. All of this dilutes the feeling of being treated as an incompetent child. Of course, care should be taken in such common situations as driving a car, not to be a back-seat driver, nor to take pleasure when a mistake has been made, and to avoid appearing to correct the partner every other second.

Disorders of Dependence

The whole aim of development is to become an adult who is reasonably autonomous, self-reliant, and self-directing. There are many people who attain intellectual and physical adulthood, but remain dependent and passive emotionally. Such a man or woman often marries an apparently domineering, assertive, competent partner, and there is a collusion between the two, as already mentioned, which can prove disastrous for the relationship when the dependent person matures and no longer needs such a strong partner. The secret of a successful outcome is for the so-called "strong" partner to realize what is going on early in the relationship and to encourage the spouse to grow up.

This means in practice that the pros and cons of a situation are always discussed and the decision is left to the dependent partner. Even more subtly, when that partner asks for advice, turn it around by asking: "What do you think?"

Every attempt should be made to engage in dialogue, but decisions should be left to the dependent person. In the same way, when they ask that things be done for them that they are afraid to do, encourage them to tackle the object of their fear rather than doing the task for them.

Independent decisions about taking initiatives, handling finances, making decisions about everyday matters, and deciding where to go on vacation should be encouraged. In general the dependent person should be supported and encouraged to tackle the things they are afraid to do, and be rewarded as they take new steps toward independence.

This is the opposite approach from the one in which the strong partner controls and regulates the life of the dependent spouse. In fact, the strong partner should not be afraid to show from the very beginning that they, too, have needs which their partner should make every effort to meet.

Disorders of Maturity

The dependent person is a frightened child. The immature spouse is an irresponsible child clothed in adult garments. These people crowd psychiatric clinics, the law courts, and the worlds of gambling and alcoholism. They have most commonly been called psychopaths. Characteristically, they need immediate gratification because they cannot tolerate frustration. They are very sensitive to criticism and have excessive and unreasonable outbursts of anger. They often resort to physical violence and are prone to sulk. They tend to lie because they are terrified of responsibility of any sort. It is out of the ranks of such personalities that gamblers, alcoholics, and the sexually irresponsible emerge. They often have unstable employment records, always promising and expecting some grand achievement, but on the whole being very poor performers with little capacity to stick to anything or to overcome difficulties. They can often be charming, promising the moon and delivering very little. They can be belligerent one moment and on their knees begging for another chance the next. Clearly not all these characteristics are to be found in the same person, but most of them show a cluster that has the unmistakable stamp of this particular type of personality.

If an attempt is made to try to cope with such immaturity, the only tenable response is kindness coupled with firmness. It has to be realized that one is dealing with an irresponsible child who is an adult. Firmness is the only way out. Such men and women have to be reprimanded for their bad conduct, told in no uncertain terms that aggression will not be tolerated, and that they will only be rewarded if they behave themselves. A certain number of such people do mature with the passage of time, but this takes hard work.

This book is not meant to be a textbook of treatment for psychological disorders, but the two conditions of anxiety and depression are so common that something has to be said about them.

Feelings of Anxiety

Mention has already been made of anxious attachment. When the anxiety is more generalized, and this is an extremely common trait, the person is apprehensive about losing their partner, their future, their prospects, and especially their health. They live their lives with constant anxiety about their survival, even though they can be, and usually are, loving, responsible, and in every other respect normal people.

When the anxiety reaches a very high level, it is accompanied by irritability, mood swings, a number of physical symptoms, and a high level of apprehension. Anxiety is a very common phenomenon, and doctors' waiting rooms are full of anxious men and women who find it difficult to cope with life.

Loving an anxious partner demands infinite patience. One moment it is time for reassurance, and the next for being jocular and getting them out of their predicament by a lighthearted approach. Anxiety cannot be ignored, but at the same time such people should be encouraged to live full lives and be helped to overcome their common fears of traveling, being away from home, or tackling new situations. They should be listened to, but encouraged to make light of their anxious preoccupations. They are often afraid of dying and while no one can guarantee certainty of life from moment to moment, such persons can almost invariably be reassured that their moment of departure has not arrived. If the symptoms become excessive, and take the form of severe phobias or obsessional manifestations, expert help must be sought.

Many spouses live happily with their anxious partners by treating their fears with care and attention, and responding to them with a mixture of gentle cajoling and humor. Today a whole array of relaxation techniques exist, including yoga and meditation, to which anxious people can resort with great advantage.

Feelings of Depression

After anxiety, the most common psychological difficulty is depression. Depression has been diagnosed since ancient times as a disorder that affects the mind, giving the person a sense of misery and gloom. It leads to lack of energy, irritability, and the desire to withdraw from life and other people, including the spouse. Today most depressive illnesses are recognized and treated successfully, usually with medication, but some are chronic in nature and very persistent.

Living with a person who is depressed can be a trying experience because of their withdrawal and apathy. They do not want to talk, go out, socialize, or be in any way available. Their partner is isolated and feels as if they are completely alone.

It is essential that the true nature of the depression is understood, otherwise the sufferer is thought to be lazy, inconsiderate, and uncaring. It is useless to pretend that they can be mobilized by being made to feel guilty, or shaken out of their lethargy. The condition is very real and debilitating.

What is needed is a combination of genuine sympathy and gentle encouragement to undertake activities and participate in events. While the withdrawal should be respected, the temperature of the water should be regularly tested and indications of a lighter mood encouraged. The spouse has to live within the reality of depression and unceasingly encourage life and activity. As with anxiety, severe depression, especially threats of suicide, should be taken seriously and professional help should be sought.

Loving entails responding accurately and sensitively to the personality of the spouse. Psychology today focuses more clearly on various aspects of the personality, although its principal features have always been recognized. In the past, however, negative behaviors were considered immoral and the person was invited to change out of fear of punishment or a sense of guilt. Both these feelings are no longer considered desirable as instruments of transformation. Instead, spouses expect to be understood, reached, and loved, and, whenever possible, to be given a second chance to restore their integrity. This is a rich field of Christian action, for loving is at the center of our faith, and love restores wholeness. In practice, there is no institution that offers as much chance for healing as the intimate relationship of marriage. So, armed with our modern psychological insights, we face a new era of healing.

This healing requires continuity, stability, and reliability, for without these the conditions do not exist for healing. Time is needed to appraise the situation, and patience is required for the appropriate response to work. Christianity has to offer the world this healing pattern against the conclusion of relationships when difficulties appear and the insistence of starting afresh with someone else. The new spouse will only produce a different set of problems. The point is stressed again and again that modern intimacy is a conflict-generating condition, and all marriages have to be continuously worked at.

8

Growing in Love

Today couples can be expected to live together for some fifty years or more. There are those who claim that no two people can endure each other for such a period, and that change is necessary. Boredom is offered as one of the reasons for divorce. In fact if a couple are offering each other the right ingredients in their social, emotional, sexual, intellectual, and spiritual life, they will not want to change. A marital relationship is a major investment of one's life, and it should not be lightly discarded if the spouse is mutually compatible. A new partner might be more exciting, but every relationship needs a good deal of effort to make it work, and so the original effort should be carefully nurtured. In addition, it is exciting to see the person with whom one lives change and grow. Loving implies that one can live with the change and assist the partner to realize their potential, in other words, be a facilitator. Of course, one of the factors that keeps the majority of couples together is children, but children eventually grow up, and the constant factor is the couple.

When it comes to describing change and growth, the one thing we are certain of is that they happen; but our understanding of the detailed mechanism of how they happen is far from complete.

At the heart of change is the life cycle of married life. This can be described as follows: the period before the first child arrives; the arrival of the first, second, or third child; entry into primary school and then secondary school; adolescence; the departure of the first child followed by the others; and then the couple return to their original dyad state. Each of these phases demands specific requirements from parents and challenges them to respond to their growing children.

There are other social and biological changes, such as entry into work, promotion, unemployment, work for both spouses, and biologically for the woman, the menopause. Another main event is moving. There are, of course, losses, particularly the death of parents, and, later on in life, of friends. These moments and changes demand appropriate responses, and they present critical moments of adaptation.

Emotionally the process of growth involves the mastering of all the features that were mentioned as belonging to the immature personality. In marriage the vital element of growth is the development of an awareness of the inner world of one's spouse. We start the intimacy of marriage much better equipped if we understand our own personality and needs. Appreciating those of our partner is the key to a successful relationship. Not only understanding, but making sure that we respond appropriately to them, is vital. This comprehension implies that we are sensitive to their moods, feelings, values, opinions, priorities, and that we respect them. Part of the process of change is that all these will slowly and imperceptibly alter with time. Thus, although the central identity of our spouse will remain the same, the details will alter, and sometimes there will be substantial change. We must not take it for granted that our partner always knows him or herself, even though they have experienced themselves infinitely more deeply than we do. Part of mutual growth is acting like a mirror to each other. We can find out what we are by the way we are responding to another person. We are also influenced by our partners, and with time we grow more like them.

We can now return to those aspects of growth that happen by degrees. We learn to delay our gratification until that of our partner is met. Both spouses can think of each other's physical needs and supply them. When finances are limited, sacrifices will be made, and the children will come first. We learn to share scarce commodities and to give up things for others. In a family, time is rarely one's own, and there are the constant demands of spouse and children. In this way, family life is a school for learning unselfishness. At the same time, family life tells us we realize that we are needed and appreciated. We sense that we have something to offer and that, however limited our capabilities, we are always trying to offer ourselves.

Such growth is never smooth. There is always the temptation to put our own priorities first, but the expectant look of a child or a spouse is a constant reminder that we are there to be available. When children are young, the end result of constant availability is fatigue, and one of the issues that faces any couple is how to meet the needs of the children without neglecting their own.

Delaying gratification, putting ourselves second, being aware of the other, and being accessible are all aspects of loving availability. Each moment becomes a chance for loving.

There is also the dark side of the relationship, the sensitivity to criticism, the conflict of disagreement, and moments of anger. Little by little we become less sensitive, we misunderstand less, we become more resilient, our patience grows, we quarrel less, and we make up more quickly. We learn to see things from the point of view of our partner and our children. We give in without feeling humiliated and defeated.

Given that our understanding of each other improves, we have to get used to each other's lapses, poor memory, untidiness (or excessive tidiness), the limitations of the menu, the many misunderstandings. If the finances are limited, and this applies to many, there is a constant struggle to make ends meet, and when there is financial flexibility some families always manage to live just beyond their resources. It is out of these circumstances that mutual tolerance and understanding grow as the partners make sacrifices for each other and their children. This is the unsung inner world of millions of families.

Coping and adapting result in mutual growth, which leads to a reciprocal respect and appreciation of each other, the hidden basis of love which makes one fond of one's spouse. There are general changes and growth processes that proceed all the time in a marriage. There are, however, more specific ones like growing emotionally, sexually, physically, and intellectually.

Growing Emotionally
Under the category of emotion, I want to describe

two processes: the reduction of idealization and the growth from dependence to independence.

As far as idealization is concerned, we have seen that during the period of courtship there is a heightened awareness of the positive aspects of our future partner. They appear to excel in intelligence, application, skills, learning, wisdom, sensitivity, and every other quality possible. When we marry, and perhaps nowadays when couples cohabit, they find the reality. The beloved is not so clever or skilled; they have problems with household tasks or challenges, are impractical, have no sense of color, are poor shoppers, short in temper, selfish, lazy, messy, and so on. Spouses have to take deep breaths when faced with the reality. What is more, they have to live with the reality. Despite how easy it is to get a divorce, spouses cannot be exchanged like cars. Idealization sometimes also holds surprises. Partners are found to have hidden talents that were not formerly known. Intimacy unfolds many buds. So the move from idealization to reality holds both disappointments and positive excitation.

The second process has been mentioned a number of times already. This is the movement from dependence to independence. Men and women start their relationships by being dependent on each other. They rely on the other for their opinions, initiatives, coping with decision making, handling finances, and so on. With the passage of time, confidence is attained, and partners want to take over areas of their lives that they had formerly handed over to their spouse. Spouses can facilitate this growth by encouraging their partner to tackle issues that they have found difficult in the past.

Partnership depends on complementarity. Spouses offer each other mutual strengths, but they can also develop additional capacities as they learn from each other.

Growing Sexually

After the initial flush of excitement, sexual activity may become less frequent, but it deepens in quality as the couple discovers what pleases them. Occasionally things go wrong when a spouse believes that sex is for conception only, and having had enough children there is no more need for sexual intercourse, but that is rare. Usually there is a deeper appreciation of the sexual dimension as the couple sees sex beyond its physical excitement to its supporting effect in their whole life.

Growing Physically

The one thing nobody can escape is the ravages of time. Partners become older and show it by graying hair, skin losing elasticity, and increased weight. It is a measure of love that spouses continue to enjoy each other even in the visible presence of such changes. There can be moments of crisis when a man or a woman enters the forties and become alarmed that they are past the prime of life. This is where loving reassurance comes into play, and they are reminded that they matter for themselves.

Another factor that may make a sudden and unexpected entry is illness. This may strike at any age, even though the majority of couples will not experience it until later in their married life. Sometimes such conditions occur early. Part of maturity is coping with such adversity.

Growing in Intelligence and Creativity

Like our physical development, our intelligence has usually reached its final form before marriage. Our IQ will not suddenly rise. But if our general intelligence is fixed, our capacity to move from intelligence to wisdom is considerable. We learn from many people and many sources, but our constant mentor is our spouse who has regular access to us. They can be our most constructive critics and help us refine our intelligence to unexpected heights.

This facilitation extends into the support we receive when we want to try a new venture at any stage in life. The new venture can be cooking, gardening, engaging in a new hobby, and even changing the course of our life by trying a new job. We need imagination and opportunity, but above all encouragement to develop hidden talents.

Change and growth are visible over time, but hard to detect day by day. In fact every moment of a life together is an opportunity to facilitate the other person, whatever the need. There is tension between self-awareness and the development of one's own needs, and the sensitive awareness and respect of our partner's needs. The usual explanation is that we are all selfish, and the only battle in life is to defeat selfishness. But psychology has shown us that what we thought was selfishness may be anxious and fearful behaviors. The sensitive awareness of this by a spouse leads to understanding and growth.

Married life is about change that enhances personal growth from immaturity to maturity, dependence to independence, idealization to reality, and facilitates the partner to engage in the same process. It takes a lifetime to get to know each other and respond accurately, but in the process, in the Christian sense, we are developing the qualities of the Trinity, in which three persons know each other perfectly and respond to each other fully. The growth of marital love is like this process and it takes a long time to achieve it. The essential accompaniments are continuity, reliability, and predictability, which have been shown repeatedly to be necessary for marital love, and are good reasons why marriage needs to be permanent if it is going to fulfill its potential.

9

Sexual Love

Sexuality, the central dynamic energy between men and women, has had a poor history in Christianity. The reasons are multiple, but three principal ones exist. The first was Greek and Stoic philosophy. Within this tradition there was a prediliction for ataraxia, which is a special freedom of the mind from the passions. Sexual arousal and the climax of intercourse were certainly emotionally agitating experiences. The orgasm was believed to cause a loss of control of reason, and at that moment human sexual activity was equated with animal activity. This disparaging view of sex as animal instinct was to have a long and profound influence on Christian theology. The loss of control of orgasm was considered to be profoundly damaging to human dignity, and people who controlled their passions were definitely superior beings.

The second element was the presence of Gnosticism and Manicheism. These were complicated movements, but central to them was the belief that the physical, the body and the flesh, trapped the spirit and the soul, and that sexual intercourse with its procreative potential was an enemy of the spirit. Marriage and sex were to be avoided. Christianity was confronted with the task of protecting marriage and yet distancing itself from sexual intercourse, although it had to testify that new life was good and to be protected in the womb. Hence abortion was considered to be gravely wrong.

The third element was the opinion of individual Greek and Latin Fathers. Among the latter, Augustine was the most influential. In his youth Augustine had known powerful sexual passion. He said to God, "Give me chastity, but not yet." There is little doubt that this strong sexual appetite played an important role in his later deliberations. He wrote on marriage, which he held to be good, and he laid down the three goods of marriage as *proles, fides, sacramentum*; or children, mutual faithfulness, and indissolubility. These three concepts, which in the Middle Ages became the goals of marriage, had a powerful and enduring impact on the theology of the Catholic Church. As far as sexual intercourse was concerned, Augustine took a pessimistic view, holding that it was always at least venially sinful, and that its only justification was the procreation of children. There was no association with love, and thus Augustine set Western theology on a false track with repercussions that are still visible today. Sexuality became inextricably linked with biology but not with love. This was an anomaly in a saint who recognized and wrote extensively about the supreme importance of love.

Later in the Middle Ages, theologians such as Aquinas modified Augustine's view on sexual passion, and indeed formulated the position that a deliberate, intended, and anticipated enjoyment of sex was right and proper. The essential link between sex and procreation, however, was maintained. This link was necessary because it had a ring of truth about it. There was no status accorded to women and their inner world, and no connection was made with human love. Attempts were made sporadically in the Middle Ages to link love with sex, although we do not know in detail how married people experienced sex. This link is urgently needed because the presence of widespread contraception and the accuracy of pregnancy with birth regulation has meant that the overwhelming majority of sexual acts are no longer procreative. Both society and the church need to find new ways to describe the significance of sexual intercourse. For many couples, only a few sexual acts are needed to produce children. In the absence of an alternative meaning, people today have adopted a hedonistic view of intercourse. Yet, these certainly are alternative meanings.

Sexual Intercourse

From the time of puberty, sexual arousal and attraction is designed for the sexual act. The sexes approach sexual arousal differently. For both, the hormone testosterone is related to sexual drive. Both men and women are aroused sexually and want to have sex, but common observation and studies show a different kind of physical urgency in men. In fact the sexuality of men is marked by physicality and that of women by affectionality. This is something that couples have to learn about each other. The man is aroused by vision, sound, and touch connected with the erotic, and up to a point, women are, too, but for the latter the "atmosphere" of the relationship counts a great deal more. The quality of the relationship matters to women, for whom the preceding hours before sex need to be affectionate and warm. Women have to accustom themselves to the physical sexual urgency of men, and men have to learn that atmosphere is important to their wives, although, of course, there are exceptions to these generalities. In so far as they hold true, it is part of the loving of the couple that they should take notice of each other's needs and try to meet them.

This challenge of love extends to the preparation for making love. Men have an urgency that drives them to make genital contact with great speed. Women may be spontaneously aroused, but often need to be caressed, stroked, hugged, kissed, and erotically excited. Here loving requires control and patience on the part of the man, and a willingness to participate in sex by the wife when she has no special desire for it. Love is now shown in the control and patience of the man, and in generosity on the part of the woman.

The same patience applies to sexual intercourse itself when the man has to hold back his climax in order to ensure that his wife reaches orgasm, too. This is a loving consideration in the very midst of the act itself. Traditional morality concerned itself with the position that the couple adopted to have coitus. One can say categorically that a couple can adopt any position that mutually satisfies them and that gives mutual erotic excitation.

During the preparation for sex and the act itself, the couple may find themselves fantasizing about each other or about impersonal erotic scenes. This intrusion of fantasies may be highly erotic, but men and women may worry whether such fantasies are legitimate, and fear that in the end they may betray their partner. We do not understand the psychology of such fantasies, which at their extreme may be sado-masochistic or have other fetishist connotations. It may be considered whether morality should have any say at such intensely private moments. The whole point of sexual intercourse is to experience and give erotic pleasure. The more personal and spouse-oriented it is the better, but at the moment the whole sexual array of individual fantasy is aroused and it cannot be easily controlled. It has to be accepted that the range of arousal, whatever its nature, is moral, provided it leads to mutually pleasurable experiences.

Throughout this book constant references are made to love having its beginning in the world of infancy and childhood. On the surface the adult sexual act appears to have no connection with that era, but this is not the case. In the process of genital interaction, the two bodies make an intimate, secure, close, rhythmic contact which is a strong reminder of the intimate closeness between baby and mother with a similar rhythm of intimacy. In fact this smooth two-in-one unity is at its best when the couple are relaxed and enjoying sex. When one or the other are alienated, they become tense, unrelaxed, and withdrawn bodily and genitally from each other, and although having sex, they are functioning as separate persons.

The conclusion of the sexual act is orgasm, which for the man almost invariably leads to exquisite pleasure accompanied by rhythmic spasm of the penis with ejection of sperm. The woman may enjoy a similar orgasmic sensation, but she might not always do so. Part of loving in these circumstances may call for the husband to manually bring her to orgasm and release the accumulated sexual tension. Whatever the method, the object of sexual intercourse is for the couple to reach mutual orgasm with its exquisite pleasure and joy.

Sexual intercourse is not always the highly exciting experience that it is meant to be. One or the other spouse may be tired, uninterested sexually, not relaxed enough, or may be submitting reluctantly to the act. For a variety of reasons, the personal closeness may be absent and the act becomes merely physical. For complete unity, the act should combine the personal component of mutual surrender and joy in each other, accompanied by physical acts. The two do not always combine, and sometimes there is just a release of sexual tension, while occasionally there is not even that. Some women have rarely enjoyed sex, particularly in previous generations when the sex act was confined to conception. So while sex can be ecstatic, it can also become routine and occasionally boring. Every effort should be made to guard it against banality, and try to make it something special because it is a symbol of the whole meaning of the encounter between spouses.

The Meaning of Sexual Intercourse

Earlier in this chapter I referred to the contemporary challenge of discovering the meaning of sexual intercourse when it is carried out for forty or fifty years after the desired family size has been attained.

The first thing to say is that the evolution of the human species has made sexual intercourse the means of perpetuating the race. There is a biological basis to sex, which at its very heart is a release from sexual tension. We would be ignoring the physical needs of men and women if we failed to acknowledge this basic dimension. But everything we know points to the fact that there is more to humanity than satisfying physical needs.

So we must move on to a more personal dimension that does justice to the sexual domain. As mentioned already, the loving dimensions of sustaining, healing, and growth need constant nurturing. It is not easy to be available, to communicate effectively, to show affection, and to negotiate conflict without the constant supply of energy and encouragement that sexual intercourse gives, and which also rewards the efforts made. The same applies to healing and growth. Responding to the woundedness of our partner means dealing with the irritable, angry, impatient, impulsive, intolerant, generally difficult part of our spouse. This requires patience, persistence, and motivation, which are in some ways supplied by sexual intercourse.

In thinking about the personal meaning of sexual intercourse, I have for some time described five individual characteristics that seem to be standing the test of time. These features, though not consciously experienced, are the existential reality of coitus, and have immensely rich personal implications. Generally what I am trying to convey with these five features is that sexual intercourse is a body language of love in which spouses are talking to each other with their bodies. What are they saying to each other?

The first communication is the acknowledgment that in allowing each other access to themselves sexually they are saying, "I recognize, want, and appreciate you. You are the most important person in my life." In this context sexual intercourse is a powerful affirmation of personhood.

Secondly, when the sexual act is performed in a fulfilling manner, the man is able to make the woman feel completely feminine and the woman can make the man feel completely masculine. Human sexuality is brought to life when the couple affirm one another's sexual identity.

Thirdly, mention has been made already of the fact that the couple will experience conflict, anger, and pain with each other. Most hurts are quickly forgotten and forgiven, but some go deeper, and the pain can be excruciating. There is much evidence that after hours, days, or weeks in pain, it is sexual intercourse that brings reconciliation. So its third feature is that it can be a reconciliatory, healing language.

Fourth, all human beings are overtly seeking meaning. We do not often spend time speculating where we come from, the meaning of life, or where we are going. In the depths of our faith we seek meaning, but we long for an answer. The knowledge that at regular intervals another human being wants us, and is prepared to celebrate life through sexual intercourse with us, is a repeated act of profound meaning in life. It is therefore an act of recurrent hope.

Finally, as human beings, we need to render thanks for our life. Sexual intercourse is the act through which we say thank you for being with me yesterday, today, and, I hope, tomorrow. It is a recurrent act of thanksgiving.

We can speculate about the meaning of sexual intercourse in a strictly spiritual sense by referring to the Trinity. The mystery of the Trinity is beyond comprehension, but it implies a total unity of three persons while they remain completely separate and unique in themselves. Attempts have been made to allocate roles to each person, such as creativity, love, and wisdom. But in the sexual act we might have a model of the total unity of two persons while each retains his or her complete separate identity. We should not forget that Paul describes the loving unity and relationship of Christ and the church in terms of marriage and the marital act. Thus sexual intercourse is the central and recurrent act that unites a couple.

What About Children?

Some may observe that in the midst of this personal expression of love the idea of children seems to be lost, and the whole tradition that has been the infrastructure of Christianity disappears with a stroke.

Those who resisted the dropping of the traditional language in the Second Vatican Council of primary and sec-

ondary ends in which the primary end was the procreation and education of children, may remind us that
they had good reason to be anxious.

Traditionalists repeat that the Second Vatican Council
said:

> Hence, while not making the other purposes of
> matrimony of less account, the true practice of con-
> jugal love, and the whole meaning of family life
> which results from it, have this aim; that the couple
> be ready with stout hearts to cooperate with the
> love of the Creator and the Saviour, who through
> them will enlarge and enrich his own family day by
> day (Pastoral Constitution, Part 2, ch. 1).

There are several observations to be made on this topic. First of all, everyone should be reminded that the
council removed the language of primary and secondary
ends. Secondly, the personal meaning of sexual intercourse goes on, whether the couple are opening their
sexual act to new life or not. What couples experience in
the act is its personal meaning, not the possible fusion
between sperm and ovum, however much they may want
a baby. Most important of all, however, is the reality that
everything we have learned about children tells us that
they need security and love, and that depends on the stability of the couple and their capacity to be loving parents. This viability of the couple and the whole welfare of
the children depends on the support that sexual intercourse gives to the parents. To stress the biology of sex is
to ignore the personal, which is its supreme value. Even
more important, remember that after the family has been
completed, there may be several decades when sexual intercourse continues. The trouble with Christian teaching
in the past is that by stressing the biological it has trivi-

alized the act. Everyone knows that sex is needed for children, and that will always remain. It is the personal that needs stressing.

Morality of Sex

It can be seen from what has been said that there is a personal morality within marriage involving sexual intercourse. One can be unloving in marriage when one takes one's partner for granted or ceases to take the trouble to make love.

Sex outside marriage was traditionally forbidden because a child might be conceived without the presence of loving parents. The advent of widespread contraception no longer motivates people in this way, although plenty of mistakes are made that often lead to abortion.

Bringing a life into the world without two parents is a grave mistake and highly irresponsible. Even more important, in light of what has been said in this chapter, sexual intercourse contains some of the deepest, personal, and loving experiences of life, and its authentic meaning can only be experienced within the context of a continuous, reliable, and predictable relationship, which is usually marriage. Making love is a powerful evocation of what true love is, and its authenticity comes into question when it is trivialized through promiscuity. The ultimate denial of its meaning is in the union of a prostitute and client when bodies meet without a personal encounter, and therefore with the total absence of love.

10

Marital Difficulties

Marital difficulties are becoming the norm in contemporary marriages. Traditionally the man was considered the head of the family, and the wife was expected to obey him. If she did not like the way things were, she had to adapt to them. In practice women resisted, defied, and used considerable emotional and sexual powers to achieve a balance, but in theory the man was in charge.

Today there is increasing equality between the sexes, and differences are often sorted out by negotiation. This works out in many marriages, but not in all. There are spouses who cannot accept that their actions are intolerable, and they persist with them. Many others see that change is needed but yet continue their unsatisfactory habits. There may be arguments and promises, but nothing is done, and so resentment and anger build up.

The difficulties that couples encounter may seem insurmountable, but in practice the common ones can be identified and dealt with. The problems can be divided into those that affect the quality of the relationship and specific problems.

Looking at the quality of the relationship, I will use a model with two sets of ideas. The first is that the marriage relationship has five main dimensions: social, emotional, sexual, intellectual, and spiritual. When the couple come together they relate on all these levels, any one of which may present difficulties. The second idea is that marriage proceeds in phases. These can cover the period before childbearing, the phase in which the first child is between the ages of one and five, when it enters school, when all the children are in primary school, when the eldest is in secondary school, when all are in secondary school, when the eldest leaves school, when all leave school, and finally leave home. Then the couple is alone again which may be for twenty years or more. Each of these stages has its own challenges, which, as we have seen, comprise the maintenance of the parents' relationship and the parenting role. For the sake of brevity, we will look at only three of these phases.

Phase one covers the first five years of marriage. This is the period when children arrive and the wife ceases working for a time. There is a new adaptation with the parents taking new roles.

The second phase is between the ages of thirty and fifty. This is the period when children are growing up, when many mothers have returned to work, and the midlife crisis occurs, ending with the menopause for the wife. By the end of this phase, the children have usually left home. These are the toughest years of marriage, combining the responsibilities of bringing up children with change in the outlook of the spouses. Change is the key word during this phase.

The third phase is between the age of fifty and the death of one spouse. This is the period when the couple return to their one-on-one state; they become a dyad once again. The children have usually left home, without necessarily interrupting their constant need for advice, money, and contact. The extended family brings grandparents, children, and grandchildren together.

A description of these common problems does not usually tell us how to solve them. Conflicts can occur in all phases of a marriage. The first thing to do is to try to evaluate the significance of what is happening. We need to distinguish between the hurts we experience at the hands of our spouses through poor memory, inattention, lapse of good manners, untidiness, impulsiveness, transient anger, which are quickly forgotten, and the dissatisfaction that affects the very core of one's being. In the latter case, we may discover that our integrity is being damaged by the restriction of our freedom, lack of love, lack of realization of our potential, and unwarranted attacks on our well-being. In other words, an essential part of our humanity is in danger.

Here is an important factor from the Christian point of view. When we are married, are we expected to suffer indignities and humiliations in order to stay married? Fundamentalist Christians say yes. For them, the state of marriage is permanent, and nothing ever excuses divorce. The Roman Catholic Church takes a very strict view on indissolubility, but nevertheless grants annulments. It is worth noting what Canon Law has to say on the subject.

The following are incapable of contracting marriage:
   1. Those who lack sufficient use of reason.

2. Those who suffer from a grave lack of discretionary judgment concerning the essential matrimonial rights and obligations to be mutually given and accepted.

3. Those who, because of causes of a psychological nature, are unable to assume the essential obligations of marriage (Canon 1095).

What are the essential obligations of marriage?

The Marriage covenant, by which a man and a woman establish between themselves a partnership of their whole life, and which of its own very nature is ordered to the well-being of the spouses and to the procreation and upbringing of children has, between the baptized, been raised by Christ the Lord to the dignity of a sacrament (Canon 1055).

The point to be taken from this Canon is that the nature of marriage is ordered to "the well-being of the spouses," which, as we have seen in the documents of the Second Vatican Council, is orientated toward love.

In other words, the spouses are entitled to look at whether their essential need for love is being met. There are, of course, differences between what the secular world considers the essentials of love, and what the church accepts, but there is a consensus that the essentials of love have to be safeguarded.

This is the clue to the way marital difficulties have to be evaluated. Is the conflict involving something essential to the concept of love for the spouse, or something non-essential? Clearly it takes time for the spouse to appreciate that a persistent problem exists that appears recurrent and unchangeable. When that moment of realization has arrived, when something fundamental is

missing or is wrong with the relationship, what should
the spouse do? This is the moment of truth. Everything
should be done to challenge the partner about the issue.
They should repeatedly be faced with it, asked to change,
cajoled, if necessary bullied and threatened. When the issue is vital, there should be no let up in the persuasion,
and this includes the assistance to change. If still no
change takes place, spouses should ask themselves whether they should seek counseling. Taking the matter outside the home is an indication of seriousness, and
sometimes makes the partner face issues that they ad-
amantly refused to look at before. If there is still no resolution to the problem, they should consider whether
they are prepared to accept the limitation and stay, or decide to separate.

What usually happens is that spouses remain frustrated
and dissatisfied for years without taking decisive action to
confront the partner. Then one day they simply pack
their bags and go. It is necessary, when a serious defect is
diagnosed, that the spouse should be confronted, and it
is with this in mind that the next three chapters were
written.

11

Phase One: The First Five Years

The first five years of marriage constitute the first phase of marriage. These years are significant in three ways. 1) They are the important years of adjustment and are loaded with difficulties. 2) It has been found that these years are very important in laying the foundations of the relationship. When a marriage breaks down, people often locate the causes in these early years. 3) It has been found that between thirty and forty percent of all marital breakdown occurs in the first five years. So they are important, and they should be supported. Let us consider the five dimensions in this phase.

1. Social Factors
Separation from parents: At the center of marriage lie

the separation of the spouses from their parents and the fusion of a new unity between husband and wife. The parents remain important and are contacted and resorted to. They remain good friends, but the spouses turn to each other for the resolution of their difficulties, management of their affairs, future planning, and the timing of children. It is natural that in all these matters they should consult each other and make mutual decisions, leaving their parents out of the consideration.

This happens with the majority of couples, but there are exceptions and this produces problems. In these instances, one or both spouses remain over-attached to parents. The wife may be over-dependent on her mother, and the husband on his father. The woman may telephone her mother several times a day or visit her at frequent intervals. The mother becomes the confidante of the daughter. The vital secrets of the relationship are entrusted to her. Instead of discussing matters with her husband, she communicates with her mother and the husband is bypassed. His opinions are ignored in favor of her mother's. The husband may turn to his father for advice on economic matters, or worse still, may be employed by his father who plays a dominant role in his son's life. Just as the daughter bypasses the husband, he bypasses her. Such a couple may be married, but they have not put aside dependence on their families.

This is a situation that leads to feelings of exclusion. Repeated requests to abandon dependence on the parent are ignored. The next phase of this problem is that the spouse is criticized, and an alliance is formed between parent and child against the spouse. The situation gets much worse with the formation of triangular tensions between parents and the partners. In the end the marriage may be terminated.

The more common problem is when a spouse is not

liked or approved of by in-laws. This puts the other partner in difficulty. They have to choose between their
spouse and their parents.

Running the household: When a couple is newly married they have to make arrangements for running the
home. Traditionally the wife has had jobs like cooking,
cleaning, and the laundry. The husband has had practical,
mechanical jobs like mowing the lawn and keeping the
car in good repair. Today there is more fluidity of roles.
The important thing is that the distribution be fair and
be experienced as such. What often happens is that the
wife, who also works outside the home, is left with all the
household chores and the care of the children. The husband may consider it sufficient to be a provider and do
next to nothing in the home. This leads to a common
problem. The wife is excessively tired and is not interested in affection and sex.

Money problems: If one listens to a cross-section of
opinion, the most common explanation for marriage
troubles is money. Money is meant to solve all the problems. The fact that no mention of it has been made up
till now is because, while money undoubtedly matters, it
is the emotional consequences that are responsible for
the conflict. There are plenty of poor people who maintain their marriages and many rich marriages that don't
work out. We have to look at the meaning of money and
its implications.

Money has three meanings. The first is its economic
value; the second is the power it gives to those who have
it; and the third is its emotional component.

The first meaning is the one that is usually considered.
This often means that there is not enough of it. Since
money is essential for buying a house, food, clothing,
and other essentials of life, its relative absence leads to
tension, quarrels, arguments, and mutual accusations.

The person who controls the checkbook has power over the partner. It is the husband who traditionally controls the money, though this is less and less true today. If a wife is dependent on her husband for her financial survival, if he does not give her enough money for the necessities, she is unable to do anything about it except go to work herself, and then she very often uses the money she earns to supplement the household budget.

In certain marriages the wife or husband may discover that the spouse cannot handle money and is irresponsible with it. This is an enormous strain on a couple. Thirdly, money has an emotional meaning. If one spouse controls it and shortchanges the other, that spouse feels unloved. He or she thinks: "If you loved me, you would share with me equally."

Another cause for conflict is housing. A young couple newly married want a place of their own. When they have to share with their families or with other couples, the scene is set for strain, and it has been found that those who start married life without an independent abode have a greater tendency toward marital breakdown.

The pressures of work: Work is important in the life of a couple for its economic value, social support, and for their self-esteem. There are two problems associated with it, however. These are working excessive hours and unemployment.

Anyone can work long hours, but it is a problem that particularly affects professional people. Doctors, lawyers, accountants, all work long hours and often come home late. This leads to constant arguments that they put their work before their home life. When they come home they are tired and unavailable for conversation. Very often they have their meal, sit in front of the television, and fall asleep. This is exceedingly irritating to the spouse. The other problem is that professional people often have to travel and leave the spouse behind. When this is frequent, it creates an emotional vacuum that is acutely painful.

Another problem is unemployment. Unemployment has a devastating effect on self-esteem and feelings of emotional availability. It is not surprising that it is associated with a high rate of marital breakdown.

Leisure hours: One of the dangers in the early years of marriage is that one of the spouses wants to enjoy the amenities of marriage: an organized household, food, and sex, without contributing to household chores. He or she might tend to use spare time to continue favorite pastimes like golf or tennis, or going to a favorite bar. A bar in particular can become a substitute home, and time spent there can easily lead to neglect of the spouse.

2. Emotional Factors

The emotional factors have been mentioned before in various parts of this book, but here I will mention them briefly again.

Loss of idealization: It has been shown that what holds a couple together in the stage of falling in love is their deep idealization of each other. In brief, each thinks the other is wonderful. Those who are wise begin to accept, even at this stage, that there are limitations to the partner. The limitations are social, as described above, or emotional, that is, in the language already used, they have shortcomings in their emotional availability, capacity to feel, be affectionate or understanding. When limitations are foreseen, their damage is limited. When not foreseen, there is acute disappointment: "This is not the man/woman I fell in love with. I can't recognize him or her." Such feelings herald profound disillusionment.

Restriction of freedom: In some instances the newly married person cannot cope with the limitations imposed on their freedom of movement and/or action. Such a person suddenly feels imprisoned, and within months of the marriage is desperately unhappy and wants to be out of it. When close attention is paid to the period of the courtship and the previous history, it will be found that he or she may have broken off the relationship more than once or been involved with previous relationships. In fact, such men or women may postpone marriage repeatedly, and once they are in it find it intolerable. Within the marriage they become depressed and withdrawn, and all they want is to get out.

Inability to cope with intimacy: The inability to cope with intimacy is another side of the few vulnerable people who marry and then regret it immediately afterward. They form the extreme pattern of avoidant attachment and cannot stand any form of closeness. They made the supreme effort to overcome their difficulty during courtship, but the continuous physical and emotional closeness of marriage is intolerable.

Immaturity: The man or woman who after marriage displays immaturity may come as a shock to the partner. There may have been indications during the courtship, but they were not interpreted correctly. The behavior consists of one or more symptoms of recurrent and acute loss of temper, excessive drinking, aggression with physical and verbal assault, inconsistent and poor work record, sexual excess, rudeness, or possessiveness. Clearly such behavior is extremely immature and endangers a marriage.

3. Sexual Problems

Non-consummation: This is a functional disturbance in which the wife experiences acute pain that makes penetration impossible. It is usually easily corrected.

Birth regulation: Most couples do not have any difficulty with birth control. They use the method most suited to them. If one spouse is a Roman Catholic, he or she may want to restrict birth control to methods acceptable to the church. There is no difficulty in finding suitable training programs to accommodate this special need.

Lovemaking: Women often experience disappointment with sexual intercourse in the first five years of marriage. They may not reach orgasm and/or may experience pain during intercourse. More commonly, there may be disappointment in the quality of lovemaking. One partner may feel that sex is not as rewarding as it was during courtship or that they don't have sex often enough. Men usually complain about frequency, and women about the ambience of the lovemaking.

Difficulty in getting pregnant: A small percentage of couples, approximately eight percent, do not become pregnant when they want to. This leads to the ordeal of examinations, keeping charts, taking fertility pills, and even proceeding to in vitro fertilization. The couple may understand with their head that it is not their fault, but they feel embarrassed about their difficulty. The husband may be found to have a low sperm count which is a blow to his self-esteem, or the wife may have hormonal difficulties. This is often a time when the spontaneity of sexual intercourse is reduced and spouses become mechanically involved in the challenge of reproduction. Their desire to conceive is intermingled with the disappointment and frustration of not being able to. This is a testing time, and the couple need encouragement to get through the difficulties.

Sexual variations: Some partners want to embroider sexual intercourse with some extra-sexual activity, such as a fetish, cross-dressing, or sado-masochistic practices. The wife, who is usually the recipient of such desires, may feel the request surprising or upsetting. The couple should seek help to understand these sexual needs.

Occasionally a homosexual man or woman marries to "cure" their homosexuality, or to prove to themselves that they are not saddled with this difficulty. To their surprise they find they cannot continue with a marriage, and to the dismay of the partner, they separate. Although such an event is exceedingly painful, it is better faced early in the marriage.

Infidelity: The early years of marriage are not usually a time when infidelity occurs. Sometimes it does, however. The affair may involve an ex-girlfriend or ex-boyfriend with whom a relationship was unresolved. As with all affairs, the pain should not stop the process of reconciliation.

4. Intellectual Challenges

A couple usually discovers common interests, outlook, opinion, in the process of the courtship or cohabitation. They will find out whether they have a common background, if their educational outlook coincides, or if they can interest one another apart from in bed. Occasionally a hasty courtship, or one based on infatuation, brings partners together who have little in common. This combination of bodies and not of minds demands an assessment of whether there is sufficient emotional and intellectual affinity to keep the spouses together.

5. Spiritual Difficulties

Couples who share the same faith tradition and who have similar spiritual values are more likely to succeed in a marriage. In mixed marriages, or in marriages in which one spouse is a believer and the other is not, conflicts can more easily arise, especially when children are involved. Couples should discuss the importance of their beliefs and values during courtship and reach a mutual understanding about this before they marry.

12

Phase Two: The Middle Years

The second phase of marriage usually occurs when couples are between thirty and fifty years old. It comprises the years when the children are growing up and careers are advancing or not. Above all, it is characterized by change of awareness and personality, which is fundamental to the survival of the marriage. Many marriages break down during these years, and the challenge of maintaining the relationship is most acute during this time.

Social Factors
The workplace: At the center of these years is the work performance of the spouses. One or the other may steadily rise up the professional ladder, and this may present

problems. The difficulties may arise from being pro-
moted to a level beyond the capabilities of the individual.
This may produce a situation in which the spouse is under stress with accompanying symptoms of poor sleep, irritability, angry outbursts, inability to relax, and finally
mood swings. The person often vents frustration on the
spouse or children. They may come to marriage counseling, thinking that there is something wrong with their
relationship when in fact the marriage is suffering from
the strain of work.

Closely associated with promotion difficulties is the
burned-out individual who exhibits similar symptoms of
strain. After years in the same job, such a person becomes
drained of ideas, energy, innovation, and a sense of despair covers all their activities. There is no point in carrying on, with frustration and irritability taking over.
This burned-out syndrome, which may be complicated
by depression, invades the family and sours relationships.
A prolonged vacation, change in work, the addition of
hobbies, or even early retirement are useful ploys in coping with such situations.

At the other end of the scale is unemployment.
Unemployment can affect everyone from senior ex-
ecutives to manual workers, and they all respond with
shock, seeing the unemployment as an attack on their
self-esteem. In particular, the person who lacks confidence in their personal relationships and relies on work
for it, finds unemployment hard to take. If their self-
esteem emanated from their work, then at a stroke they
are rendered impotent as people. Their power base evap-
orates, and their single most important reason for existing disappears. In their own eyes they become
worthless because their position, status, and money were
linked to their identity. They find it difficult to recognize
value in themselves, and they withdraw in a state of an-

ger, resentment, despair, or futility. In this heightened plight of irritability they pick quarrels, turn to drink, fail to look after themselves or their family, feel sad or distressed, and cannot take initiative. There is good evidence that unemployment increases the incidence of marital breakdown.

The spouse of an unemployed person needs to assure the partner that he or she still matters, whether they have a job or not. This is a hard task that has to be expressed in affection, sex, encouragement, and reassurance. Keeping up hope of re-employment is vital, even if there is a diminished opportunity for it. Above all, allowances have to be made for their sensitivity and inability to respond in a relaxed manner.

During these years men and women find themselves in a position of uncertainty about their future. They may not be advancing or receding, but standing still, uncertain where to go next. Such indetermination puts pressure on the spouse to make all the decisions. The partner should refuse this. The choice of staying, leaving, or changing careers is something that only the individual should decide. The best thing the spouse can do is to help the partner evaluate the situation. Are they doing what they want to do in their present job? Are they being fulfilled? Are they realizing their potential? Are they rightly or wrongly resentful at the way they are being treated? These and similar questions should be considered together, but the final decision regarding future choice should be placed squarely on the shoulders of the person whose job is involved.

Children in the family: This second phase of marriage covers the period when the children are growing up. From about the age of seven or eight, young people will challenge the authority of the parents. They will want to know why the parents are asking or demanding certain behavior, and they will judge it according to the criterion of fairness. The whole sense of justice and fairness will begin to arise from this age onward. Parents cannot get away with naked authority, and they have to justify their demands and behavior. Children are outraged if they feel their parents are behaving in an authoritarian way.

As puberty begins, there is a need to treat the adolescent as an adult in miniature, both emotionally and sexually. This is the time when parents will be absorbed with the responsibility of protecting their children from the dangers of too much freedom socially, emotionally, and sexually. If they are not careful, they will be divided in their expectations, and these years can become tense for the spouses. Adolescents can one moment behave like an adult, and the next like a child, and this confuses parents. One spouse may incline toward harsh discipline, and the other toward softness. The anxieties of the spouses may be projected on each other and lead to quarrels about the best way of controlling the situation. Smoking, drinking, dress, staying out late, school work, may all become issues needing a combined approach in which the parents have to think and act together.

Emotional Factors
From dependence to independence: One of the major shifts during these years has already been mentioned, but it bears repeating because it is crucial to contemporary marriage. This is the movement from emotional dependence to independence. Couples often start marriage very dependent on one another, relying on one another for opinions, values, ideas, and initiatives. This pattern goes on for a number of years, and then imperceptibly one or both spouses want greater independence.

What follows is vital for the marriage. If the other spouse offers encouragement, the move from dependence to independence proceeds smoothly and advantageously for both partners. The alternative is for one spouse to see the other's growth as a threat. Instead of welcoming initiatives, they block them. Every effort is frustrated. This makes the other spouse angry, and they begin even more to do their own thing, and refuse to submit to the other's will. There are ensuing quarrels and arguments. This inability to facilitate the development of the other expresses insecurity. Counseling can help to explain what is going on in the relationship, and what changes are needed. If the changes do not take place, the spouse trying to grow may look elsewhere for someone who appreciates his or her growing talents and initiatives and gives unconditional acceptance.

From insecurity to security: A number of spouses start their relationship with the anxiety of being abandoned and the fear of authority. The fear of being abandoned is deeply ingrained in their attachment behavior. They expect to be abandoned for no obvious reason, or they feel unlovable and unwanted. This fear leads them to behave in an appeasing manner, giving into all the whims of the spouse. If the spouse is emotionally and sexually demanding, the partner will give in and try to please, even when this puts them under constant strain.

They work on the principle: "I know I am not good enough for you, and you may give me up at any moment. I can never succeed in pleasing you completely, but I will do all I can to satisfy you. If I go on pleasing you, you may decide not to abandon me." This insecurity, like dependence, may change with time. The spouse may find their own security through success in their own life or through an affair which makes them feel wanted or appreciated.

The result of such a change is that they will become less concerned with pleasing their spouse and more interested in satisfying their own priorities. The spouse will notice the change and become alarmed at the loss of caring concern. Their anxiety will rise at the meaning of this change, which they will interpret as a loss of interest in them, and they will put pressure on the spouse to revert to previous habits. This will not happen, and quarrels and arguments will follow.

The shift from insecurity to security is often accompanied by a growth of self-esteem. The same applies to the development of independence from dependence. This self-esteem yearns for recognition and appreciation. The emerging person wants to cease being the one who gives adulation, to wanting to receive it. There is a whole reversal of emotional exchange and this utterly confuses the couple. All they know is that they are no longer behaving in the customary way. The developing person challenges the partner, defies him or her, refuses to placate, and takes on a new strength of character.

The same applies when the insecurity stems from fear of authority. Gradually figures of authority are no longer alarming or frightening, and so the frightened spouse stands up and challenges them. The challenge may be the refusal to cook, mow the lawn, keep prearranged commitments, or do what they are told.

Changes from insecurity to security may cause an upheaval in a marriage as the spouses change in their behavior without realizing what is happening. The change needs explaining to make sense of it.

Lack of awareness of a spouse's problem: The whole of this book has been written with the experience of thirty years of counseling and seeing couples in action. When a couple is in the midst of a changing relationship, they may not be aware or clear about what is happening to them. They will come to the counselor with a story of escalating arguments, the certainty that one or the other, or both, are changing, or there is a growing indifference. It is the arguments or the indifference that are couched in moral language that hits the consciousness of partners. They are told by their spouse that they are selfish, lazy, self-centered, egotistical, proud, drunk with success, intolerant, or uncaring, because they do not understand the problem and the change that is taking place.

It takes a lot of insight to appreciate that a partner is changing and needs something different from you. The same applies to oneself. It takes a lot of time to recognize that one is changing from dependence to independence, from insecurity to security, from self-rejection to self-acceptance, which makes one less frightened, guilty, compliant, placating. In particular, if one does not recognize these changes as valid, one may be influenced by the criteria of one's partner, and feel that one is a bad spouse for wanting these changes or failing to recognize the legitimacy of particular changes.

The trouble is that if one spouse has been angry or unhappy for a long time, when the time comes for change, that spouse may just want to get away. We take a long time to appreciate what is happening to us and our partner, and that an issue vital to our personality is at stake. In the end we are furious that our spouse did not detect our need earlier on and respond to us when we were ready to receive their efforts.

The most common example is the wife whose husband is demanding, wants frequent sex, his meals prepared, and the house clean. He gets angry at the slightest irritation and is jealous and possessive, refusing his wife any freedom at all. Then the wife gains confidence and declines to give in to his demands. All hell breaks loose. He is verbally and physically abusive, but she stands her ground and refuses to yield. Her time has come. She turns down sex, she may not cook for him, she goes out with her own friends, and begins to put the husband second in her priorities. Suddenly the husband realizes that he is losing, and he begins to be conciliatory. At this point he expects his wife to praise him for his conversion and return to her previous behavior, but she does not. She is furious with her husband, and cannot easily be reconciled to his changed approach. He becomes dejected and despairing, and turns back to his old habits of coercion to try to get the concessions he wants.

This is a standard picture in counseling situations, brought about by changes in one spouse, often the wife. Either partner may have been anxious, frightened, or feel guilty at the beginning of the relationship, and act out of these emotions. It takes years for them to gain independence, sensitivity, and self-esteem, and to recognize that they are behaving to their own disadvantage. When they assert themselves, they have to work through the onslaught of their spouse who makes them feel either guilty or angry for their new approach. Finally they have to overcome these feelings and turn to counseling, or even sometimes to the police and a lawyer, to get away from their partner and seek justice for themselves and their children. Very often they are so disgruntled in this process and so angry that they do not want anything to do with the spouse who has put them through such a trial. That is why so many do not come to counseling, or only do so to get a stamp of approval for terminating a relationship. After so many years of struggle, they give up hope of their spouse ever changing, and they realize that they want a different partner. That is why what is advocated in this book is the examination of marriages at regular intervals so that changes may be recognized at an early stage, when counseling or intervention may still be effective.

Sexual Problems

The second phase of a marriage is often the period when sexual problems emerge. The first phase is imbued with hope that the initial difficulties will be overcome, and they often are, but if not, problems persist and worsen.

First of all, there may be lack of affection and no preparation for intercourse and its associated pleasures. Husbands or wives are often not good lovers, and both affection and intimacy are difficult to negotiate. These couples may remain together and have sporadic sex, which is carried out for the sake of relief from sexual tension. Such couples proceed year after year with a poor sex life.

A recurring pattern is one in which the man agrees to come for counseling because he shows very little interest in sex. A physical examination shows no abnormality. What emerges is that the wife is aggressive and dominating, and puts her husband down at regular intervals. He is compliant outwardly, but rages with anger and resentment inwardly. The result is that he does not approach his wife for weeks or months at a time. The absence of sex and affection makes the wife even more belligerent, and a vicious cycle of anger, frustration, and poor sex is established. These patterns need to be recognized in order to interrupt them.

The most common sexual difficulty in this phase is that the couple might be faced with an episode of infidelity, which has to be placed in the proper context. Is it a one-night stand of pure sexual attraction? Is it an expression of erotic and personal significance, without threatening the relationship, or is the affair an indication of a terminal rejection of the marriage? Very often the first variety is not communicated to the partner unless a venereal disease is involved, which of necessity affects the spouse. The second pattern is sooner or later found out, and is either brought to an end slowly or suddenly, or tolerated. The third variety has a way of terminating by the very nature of events.

In most instances of infidelity there is no reason for terminating the marriage (see chapter 15 for more on this). There is a need for forgiveness, but even more important, to go beyond forgiveness, which is to go beyond anger at being displaced, the frustration of what the third party is providing, and the lack of trust to understand the contribution of the so-called innocent party. Beyond forgiveness means that there is a need to understand the conscious, and as far as possible unconscious, emotional and sexual requirements of the partner who has had the affair and try to meet them. This is in opposition to the old-fashioned view that only the adulterer or adulteress is in the wrong, should show repentance and a firm commitment to mend their ways. This is a morality based on self-control which has its own value but has been superseded by one in which we need to understand what motivates human beings and try to reach out to the depths of their being.

Intellectual Challenges

Changes during this phase usually involve the transformation of opinions, attitudes, and values. The idealization of youth may be replaced by the cynicism or reality of middle age. The reality of the first half of life may be softened by an awareness of the needs of our neighbors. Couples may become alienated from each other as one becomes more cynical, harsh, trusts people less and less, and feels that the only policy is that of self-preservation, clashing with the altruistic intentions of the partner.

Political views may change, but these do not often account for conflict in a marriage. Spouses usually agree to differ on such issues. What matters is a change of attitude that involves altering the whole way of life. A spouse may decide to give up banking, medicine, legal work, and take up gardening or acting. This means a whole upheaval of the family, not for business reasons but for aesthetic ones. Views may change on politics, morality, the meaning of life and its priorities. There may be clashes as the husband becomes more materialistic, or the wife wants to enjoy the quality of life. These clashes of outlook are rarely severe enough to damage a marriage, provided the social, emotional, and sexual relationship is good.

Spiritual Difficulties

With the advent of large-scale ecumenism, the religious differences between couples are largely negotiated with goodwill and equanimity. There may be an occasional episode in which a spouse becomes overtly religious and spends a great deal of time in church. Occasionally they join a movement which is intolerant of outsiders, and the spouse is placed on the fringe of the partner's priority, but these are rare situations.

Another source of conflict may be differing attitudes on the upbringing of children from the point of view of religion. This may become a heated matter, but once again is rarely likely to lead to serious conflict.

One point needs mentioning, which is that during these two decades either spouse may stop going to church, may become agnostic or even atheistic. Such a change may be very distressing to the other spouse and a major upset in confidence, but it is not usually a serious source of marital conflict.

13

Phase Three: The Later Years

The third phase of marriage continues from the age of fifty to the death or departure of one spouse. This is a period that may last twenty to thirty years or even more. The extended third phase is a phenomenon of our century, and we do not know a great deal about it except that marital difficulties, separation, and divorce continue into it. The majority of difficulties are a continuation of the ones seen in the second phase, but there are a number of specific issues that arise in this third phase.

Social Factors
The main phenomenon of the third phase is the departure of the children. That is not to say that the children who leave do not continue to contact the parents, come to stay with them, use them for support, and, when

they have their own children, use them as babysitters. All this happens and brings about the integrating of the three generations. At its best this extended family milieu is one of the cohesive forces in society transmitting values, opinions, and religion from one generation to the next. At a time when community is hard to find, this extended community is probably one of the most powerful integrating elements in western society.

All this is the positive side of the picture. There is a negative side as well. This happens when the children are alienated from their parents and do not meet or contact them. This is exceedingly painful for parents who have devoted so many years to bringing them up. Sometimes the arrival of grandchildren may melt the ice, but even then obstacles remain.

As far as the couple themselves are concerned, the departure of the children returns them to the dyad of the first phase of their marriage. Normally they return to a relaxed, unencumbered state with more free time to enjoy each other's company and to take trips. This is a time to revitalize the intimacy that may have been diluted in the second phase of marriage. Increasing good health allows the majority of couples to enter old age enjoying companionship, intimacy, and, as we shall see, sex.

Once again this is the positive side. There are couples who on losing sight of their children, wake up to find that they are strangers. They may find they have little in common after the children have left, and they simply separate. They may or may not divorce. On close questioning, one finds that the emotional and sexual separation existed even before the children had left. The spouses were simply waiting for the departure to finalize a break that sometimes began at the start of marriage.

When the alienation is mutual, there is little pain in this split, but when one partner is still emotionally attached, there can be a great deal of distress. The attached spouse has to mourn the departure of their partner. If they hate being alone, their loneliness may lie heavily on them.

Twenty percent of marriages break up in this phase, and we have to learn a great deal more about the causes, but one point which I have mentioned already needs stressing, namely that a healthy emphasis on the couple means that when the children depart there is a residual resilience which holds them together in the absence of the unifying force of the offspring.

Emotional Factors

One of the reasons why couples break up during this phase is that, even at this late stage, emotional transformations are taking place. The husband or wife is moving from dependence to independence, from insecurity to security, from lack of self-esteem to self-acceptance, with the consequence that they outgrow the partner.

Sometimes we find men and women in middle age who have failed to be rebellious, independent, or to enjoy themselves in their youth. Study, work, or an early marriage kept them at their desk or at home with massive responsibilities. As these duties disappear, they might have a fling during this period. They may drink too much. They may have an extramarital relationship of a longer duration, knowing well enough that they will not leave their spouse. They build a new life as they emotionally realize characteristics of youth, initiative, sexual and erotic excitation and fun, which are associated with youth. They astonish their spouse, children, and relatives by acting in what appears to be an irresponsible manner, but which for them is the capturing of the first spring of life. Within the Catholic church, a similar feature of late maturation can be seen in priests who leave in their fifties and sixties to marry for the first time.

This late emotional development can leave behind an amazed and thoroughly unhappy partner, and astonished children who have acquired a parent who doesn't act his or her age.

Sexual Problems

The clearest biological manifestation of this phase is the advent of menopause which occurs at about the age of fifty. Ovulation ceases, and so does the monthly period, and it heralds the end of procreation, but not of sexual intercourse, which can go on for twenty or thirty years. This is the clearest indication that no inevitable link between sex and reproduction exists. The main purpose of sexual intercourse is the unity and love of the couple, and the fact that this feature was absent from the mainstream of theology for two thousand years of Christianity is a great defect in its thinking.

The menopause itself does not interfere with sexual intercourse, which can proceed uninterrupted. Many women experience adverse symptoms at menopause: sweating, flushes, insomnia, irritability, loss of energy, and may offer these as excuses for avoiding sex. Studies show that in those instances where women experience sexual difficulties at the menopause, these existed beforehand, and are not specifically caused by it. When the symptoms are really unpleasant, replacement hormonal therapy can be used with advantage.

The main discovery of the last half century is that sex can be enjoyed and continued long after menopause. The main problem against the continuation is male impotence. Studies from the time of Kinsey have shown that impotence, which is to date irreversible, rises during this phase in an accumulative manner and is the single most serious constraining factor.

During this period extramarital affairs may continue.

In the second phase of marriage, both men and women can become anxious in their mid-life crisis, and seek extramarital relationships to reassure themselves that they are still attractive sexually. This need continues in the third phase, and affairs continue to occur. The reasons may be for purposes of reassurance, a continuation of a trend that started early in married life, a late flourishing of youthfulness, a late emotional development, or an exploration of eroticism in a marriage that had become indifferent. Each instance has to be understood and explained to the spouse. Depending on what category it is, the marriage may or may not survive.

Intellectual Challenges

The principal feature of this third phase is the good health enjoyed physically and intellectually by the couple, but there may be a few people whose intellect deteriorates. The single most important aspect of cognitive damage is to the memory. Many elderly people become forgetful and in this way cause distress to their spouse.

Large-scale intellectual deterioration accompanies Alzheimer's disease, and one of the most distressing aspects of this third phase is when one partner becomes gradually affected. Initially this is confined to loss of memory, poor recall of names, which causes acute distress to the individual. A great deal of love is required to go on caring for an intellectually deteriorating partner.

Another feature of old age is the development of paranoid attitudes. A certain number of elderly people become obsessed with their possessions (which they believe are stolen), feel they are disliked, believe plots are arranged behind their backs for their destruction, feel threatened by poisoning, and they can put all this down to their spouse who, in the absence of a medical interpretation, feels very hurt.

Spiritual Difficulties

As the years pass and death looms, a certain attitude about the next life has to be struck. Most people concentrate on the here and now, and do not bother about death. Others are preoccupied with it, and spiritual help may be needed. But the most powerful answer in marriage is a life lived in love, with the abiding conviction that God is love and a life based on love will continue in the next world.

14

Sexual Difficulties

At the heart of sexual intercourse is the meeting between the personal and the erotic. This is a statement that needs clarifying. Mention has been made that childhood is the first intimate relationship of personal love, and marriage is the second one. This means that if there are problems in the personal dimension in the first intimate relationship, they will appear in the second and may focus in the sexual act.

Either partner may emerge with difficulties of intimacy through an avoidant attachment, that is, getting close to another person may be difficult and the intimacy of sexual intercourse highly threatening. Such a person finds closeness, all forms of closeness, difficult, and so the sex act is particularly challenging.

Much more common is the emergence of a man or a woman who feels emotionally deprived. They experience the feelings of not being sufficiently loved, wanted, or appreciated. This can apply to either partner and when sex takes place, they do not enjoy it because they feel used and not loved. This is a very common sexual problem, particularly for women who often say, "All you want is my body, not me." Such a person has real difficulty in feeling wanted for themselves. Initially the sexual attraction they feel may give them a sense of being loved and they respond to it with alacrity. Interestingly enough, such people may approach sex with a passionate desire for it in the courtship period. When they marry, they may lose interest in sexual intercourse and become disenchanted with it.

The partner is astonished. A few months ago they were making passionate love; now their spouse is no longer interested, and they fail to understand the transformation. The alternative behavior is for the deprived individual to continue making love with high frequency as a way of meeting emotional needs. This applies to both sexes, but particularly the man who may find it difficult to reach his wife emotionally and uses sex as a substitute for affection. There are special difficulties when there is a combination of two emotionally deprived people in which the husband uses sex as an instrument of meeting his deprivation, and the wife, instead of feeling loved, considers herself used in the process. This is a particularly devastating form of incompatibility.

Psychologists take the view that sometimes the sex act is a way of exercising power over the partner. The husband or the wife who feels neglected, ignored, unimportant in the general sense of the word, feels that when it comes to sex they have power in their hands that they can exercise over the partner. The wife, who feels ill-used or mistreated, may exert power over her husband by allowing or withholding sex.

Independently of this hold over the partner, it is claimed that there is something particularly energizing in sexual intercourse, and at the simplest level the macho man may feel that in being involved with sex he shows mastery over his wife who has given in to his powerful seductive powers. Feminist writers see the power struggle of the sexes culminating over coitus in which the man seduces and the woman submits. When a couple is relating at the level of power, authority, and submission, loving feelings may evaporate. Sex participates in the struggle for conquest and is no longer a freely loving donation of oneself. At the extreme end, such a power struggle becomes sado-masochistic in the widest sense of that word.

The weak person, most often the wife, gives in to sex to please her husband, to keep him satisfied, to keep him quiet. Sex becomes a price to pay. In this sense when women are not emancipated, they use the sex factor to buy attention, but this is no exchange of love, and sex becomes a bargaining ploy. There can be little doubt that the free exchange of sexual love is an infinitely better basis for marital love than coerced sex, whatever the basis for coercion.

The Effects of Anger

Another personal factor that intervenes in the readiness to have sexual intercourse is anger. Anger may be caused by any reason. Thus spouses can get angry because they feel their trust has been betrayed, their independence is not respected, they are not appreciated enough, are ignored, are not doing enough for the family, or some special request is ignored. They may be behaving irresponsibly or uncaringly. These are long-term issues. There may be short-term ones of rudeness, anger, sarcasm, ridicule, or humiliation, which may upset the partner. When a spouse is angry the natural reaction is to retaliate or withdraw from intimacy, including sexual intercourse.

One of the recurrent difficulties that couples experience is that one spouse is angry and the other seeks forgiveness or wants reconciliation, expecting immediate sex. This happens often, but sometimes the angry person cannot put aside their hurt and pain immediately. They need time to get over their resentment. Their partner, who is impatient, does not appreciate this delay, and tension arises over the misunderstanding.

The above are psychological difficulties that alienate the couple at the personal level. There may be social ones as well. The social factors may affect their sex, but they usually weigh more heavily on the woman. There are three such social influences. The first is the attitude that sex is for conceiving children and when the desired size of the family has been completed, there is no more need for sexual intercourse. This attitude was strongly reinforced by the church's position, which at its worst gave the impression that all that marriage required was to have children, and the more the better. One would think that such a view has become obsolete, but there are still some people who hold tenaciously to it.

The second attitude is that sex is for men and that all women have to do is please them. The relatively stronger physical sexual drive of men, their apparent need to have sex more often, their difficulty in being affectionate, all add to a picture that men want one thing only, and are prepared to have it at any cost. It is women's emancipation that has made it increasingly clear that women also have sexual needs, which are physical but also require an affective component. Women need to feel loved as persons as well as sexually, whereas some men are quite happy when their physical needs are satisfied.

The third social factor, which has psychological over-
tones, is that sex is dirty. Here the attitude of the parents
is particularly important. It can convey the feeling to the
child that sex is dirty and guilt-ridden. In previous generations, when there were powerful taboos on sexuality
and children were warned against masturbation, some
people grew up with a powerful sense of discomfort over
sexual matters. Sex and guilt were so intimately linked
that any expression of sex felt forbidden. Such links between sex and guilt may have been associated at home
with no conversation on sexual matters. Nakedness may
have been frowned upon, and the young person emerged
from childhood with a combination of ignorance and dis-
taste for the subject.

Of course it is possible that there may be physical
problems with sexual arousal and the experience of sexual
pleasure that are camouflaged by social explanation. Thus
a spouse who does not enjoy sex for biological reasons,
which are not understood, hides behind an acceptable social taboo.

Thus at the personal level it is possible that a couple
may experience difficulties from psychological and social
reasons that inhibit them from wanting or enjoying sex.

This personal side has to be united with the erotic
one. The erotic dimension comprises desire, arousal, intercourse, and the aftermath. It has been suggested several times already that men appear to have a more powerful
sexual drive than women, which can be aroused at any
time. We are learning that women also have sexual needs,
and in individual circumstances these are as powerful as
those of men, although intensity fluctuates over the
monthly sexual cycle. In most women, sexual desire is
linked with the mood.

The Importance of Atmosphere

When the atmosphere is cordial, affectionate, and understanding, and consideration is shown, a woman is more ready to respond erotically. The popular myth is the picture of a dinner for two with candles and roses, giving a very private and emotional exchange. This may work, but the background relationship is important for a woman. Does she feel her husband is in touch with her, understands and/or appreciates her? This is the background against which sexual intercourse should take place.

But, if the mood is right, there is still the phase of arousal. Here mutual excitation is desired. The man wants his genitals touched, and the wife her breasts, clitoris, and vagina raised to a level of excitation. This foreplay is an important part of the sexual act. The man may simply ignore it and ask for penile intromission right away, not be familiar with the wife's preferred arousal site, be too forceful and rough with his hands, or go through a cursory fumble and expect his wife to respond immediately. In the absence of appropriate foreplay, the wife may be totally uninvolved during sexual intercourse, praying that it will soon be over, or even counting the cobwebs over the bed. There are women who become excited at the slightest touch, and are aroused with the greatest ease, for whom foreplay is no problem, but the majority of women, and many men as well, need to be aroused so that they can enjoy sexual intercourse.

The act itself should last sufficiently long so that the couple enjoys mutual orgasm, even if it is not simultaneous. We shall see below that some women fail to ever reach orgasm, and some may not reach it every time. When the act has gone well, the pleasure of being in sexual contact with each other is satisfaction enough. As mentioned already, in some instances the husband may have to induce orgasm manually to relieve the sexual tension of his wife. A much rarer problem is the occasional situation when the husband has an orgasm but cannot ejaculate sperm.

The aftermath of sexual intercourse is a highly pleasurable, enjoyable experience in the arms of each other, or in close contact. Some wives complain that after the husband has reached his climax, he turns over and goes to sleep. If the wife has not had an orgasm, being left high and dry is not conducive to a loving aftermath. In any case, the period after the intense pleasure is one to be shared together. The whole point of sexual intercourse is togetherness.

All these points can be corrected, and an effort be made to make sexual intercourse a genuine experience of mutual affection. The success of intercourse is obtained when the personal and the erotic are in tune and fuse with one another. Clearly they will not do so when there are the difficulties described above, but even in the absence of these problems, sex may be carried out when the couple are tired, tense, irritable, or in some way distracted by outside events. They may be making love and be preoccupied with money, business worries, illness, the children, or some aspect of the future. In these circumstances, sex will not be relaxed or satisfactory. Thus, not every act of sexual intercourse will be perfect. Some will be far from perfect, but at the very heart there will be an attempt at closeness.

A particularly distasteful aspect of sexual intercourse is one in which one spouse is drunk or under the influence of drugs, and yet insists on having sex. This can be a degrading experience and is no act of love.

Deterioration in a Relationship
The above difficulties often exist in the presence of a

good and loving relationship. When a personal relationship begins to deteriorate, this is often reflected in less frequent, unsatisfactory, or absent sex. The complete cessation of sex is often a symptom that something is seriously wrong.

Patterns of serious marital disturbance arise when a person who married for the need of security gradually discovers that they no longer need their partner to rescue them. The same applies to relationships which start on a basis of dependence and the spouse has outgrown emotional dependence on the partner. The same is true, too, of relationships where dominance and submission have existed, and the submissive person matures and no longer needs to be dominated by the spouse. There are other relationships in which the partner is not affectionate enough, is too aggressive or dismissive, is not remotely sensitive to one's needs. In these situations, the deprived spouse does not feel loved enough. This is particularly the case when a spouse has a wounded childhood, grows up feeling unloved, and responds to the signals of a cold, unloving partner who is accepted on the basis that they continue the disturbance of childhood.

In all these situations the withdrawal from sex is accompanied by a feeling that they are no longer interested emotionally in the partner. Such men or women talk of "falling out of love." In the terms used in this book, they have become detached emotionally from the spouse. Attachment is the means by which the relationship has been formed, and as long as the emotional attachment continues there is a bond that sustains the couple. When that goes, they remain in the relationship out of habit, for the sake of the children, for religious reasons, because they cannot stand being alone, or because they cannot cope with the stress of terminating the relationship. However, there is not a viable emotional relationship, and sex ceases or becomes very infrequent.

Such sexual withdrawal in the absence of residual emotional interest spells the death of the marriage. There is a shell in which the couple lives, eats, and sleeps together, but the relationship is not viable. When this occurs, the marriage is essentially over, and sexual difficulties are the symptom for their non-existent relationship.

Biological Basis for Loss of Sexual Interest

There is, of course, a biological basis for loss of sexual interest. The most common is a post-puerperal depression. A small number of women become depressed after the birth of a child. The depression may be short-lived, a few days or a few weeks, or it may be more severe and last months. During this time the woman often loses her sexual feelings and has no desire for intercourse.

Depression is common in women, and may strike at other times, too. When a woman is depressed, she may lose her desire for sexual intercourse. This loss is also expressed by a man when he is depressed. Sexual desire is closely connected with the hormone testosterone, and when this is missing for any reason sexual desire may be lost. Prolonged pain from any source may be sexually incapacitating, and both men and women who are affected by rheumatoid conditions may find sex difficult.

Sexual Abuse

In the past decade a great deal of attention has been given to sexual abuse of children, which is significantly prevalent. It is quite clear that such an experience in childhood can leave scars on the adult. Most sexual abuse is perpetrated on young girls, but boys can suffer as well. Young girls can be abused by their fathers, stepfathers, and brothers. Little boys can suffer at the hands of their mother, siblings, occasionally the father, or even a respected person like a priest.

The person who has been abused approaches sex with the feeling of having been exploited rather than loved. They know the meaning of betrayal, and their trust in people is low. They have suffered pain, embarrassment, distress, and humiliation sexually, and their adult experience is a mixture of hope and anticipated dread. They hope that this time they will be loved, desired, and not used as an object of abuse. If their partner is conscious of their hurt, and their approach is sensitive and delicate, healing can take place. If, on the other hand, the abused person is approached with sexual indifference, their anticipated dread is confirmed.

Sexual Dysfunctions

These problems have attracted a great deal of medical attention in the past twenty-five years. Several textbooks deal in great detail with these difficulties. Only the briefest mention will be made here.

Non-consummation affects about one percent of couples. In this instance the woman finds it very difficult or impossible to allow penetration, and at the moment the orifice of the vagina, indeed the whole vagina, goes into spasm and the penis meets a wall of resistance. Pushing against this resistance is extremely painful, and is naturally resisted. The husband retreats and tries again, but now the wife expects to be hurt and her resistance is doubled. This sets up a vicious circle, and the difficulty is reinforced, leading to non-consummation.

Couples can go to sexual clinics for this problem, or they can seek help with a fertility clinic. The remedy is usually simple. The wife is helped to learn how to relax her muscles, including the vagina. When this is achieved, the woman introduces dilators into her vagina which are there to help her tolerate a penis-like object without pain and remain relaxed while she is doing it. Gradually she introduces dilators of larger size, and in due course, her finger. All the time she is gaining confidence that she can tolerate an object, and her husband may assist by introducing the dilators himself. Finally anxiety is overcome, and the couple can try active intercourse, usually with success.

In the male there are two common functional problems. One is impotence and the other is premature ejaculation. There are at least two forms of impotence, primary and secondary. Another description of it is erectile dysfunction, that is, the inability to have an erection or to maintain it after intromission. Primary impotence, which is rare, suggests that the man has never had an erection, while in secondary impotence the man has been successful but fails on some occasions. There are many reasons for impotence, including physical and psychological causes. The most common is some form of apprehension in which the man becomes nervous about the occasion, the person with whom he is having sex, or the feelings that are aroused by the sexual occasion. The anxiety plays havoc with the nervous system that supplies the penis, and the blood engorgement which is responsible for the erection is not sustained. Secondary impotence can often be helped and sufferers are encouraged to seek help from a specialist in sexual dysfunctions.

The other common male sexual dysfunction is premature ejaculation. In this situation the man ejaculates too soon. Sometimes the orgasm with the ejaculation takes place even before intromission occurs, or very soon after the penis has entered the vagina.

The obvious problem is that the wife is not given time to be sexually excited before the husband ejaculates and brings intercourse to an end. Sometimes the answer to premature ejaculation is to wait for a short while and to have intercourse again soon afterwards. This second time the penis may remain erectile for a longer period before the climax. Another form of traditional treatment is for the wife to place her thumb and forefinger at the tip of the penis and apply pressure. This stops the desire to ejaculate and after the feeling has subsided intercourse can restart. This process of stop and restart may be helpful for premature ejaculation.

As far as the woman is concerned, two common problems are dyspareunia, which is the experience of pain during sexual intercourse, and anorgasmia, failure to have an orgasm. These two dysfunctions are associated with the specific fears that women have in relation to intercourse, and the same problems as men which are excessive anxiety and the inability to relax. The ability to relax is related to vaginal flaccidity and orgasmic response. Both these problems are complex and need specialized attention.

The treatment of sexual dysfunction depends basically on discussion with the individual and the couple so that the specific problem can be related to past and current sexual trauma. There is, of course, a range of physical treatments that try to reverse organic problems.

"Talking therapy" is a way that an individual or a couple can come in touch with their memories and feelings over sexual matters. Individuals may have been abused in their childhood, witnessed painful sexual scenes, or experienced sexual trauma in adult life. These painful moments may cause the person to anticipate a repeat of the distress, causing them to be anxious and want to avoid sex in any form. Talking about it brings the incident into focus and gradually empties it of the hurt and upset it is eliciting. Thus there is a mental strengthening which allows the person to face the frightening sex with a new resilience.

The above therapy is often combined with the Masters

and Johnson approach which has been in operation for two decades. This is a way of desensitizing the couple to sexual fears by encouraging them to approach sexual intercourse step by step. The couples are told not to have any sexual intercourse for a given period of time. This gives them relief from the pressure to perform sexually, which has become very distressing to them. The first step they are advised to take is to have a bath and then luxuriate in touching and rubbing each other with some aromatic lotion on the non-erotic parts of their bodies. The aim of this exercise is to give pleasure which is nonsexual, but it helps to relax them in close proximity to each other. In this way they become used to physical intimacy, and can be close to each other in a relaxed state. If they get aroused sexually, they are instructed to ignore this.

The next step is to proceed along the same lines and touch each other in the erotic parts of their body, the breasts, clitoris, vagina, the penis and any other part which is sexually exciting. The aim of this phase is to encourage the couple to be able to enjoy each other sexually in a relaxed state. Again they are told not to proceed to sexual intercourse.

The next step is to encourage the couple to repeat the first two steps for relaxed contact and erotic pleasuring, which then proceeds to penile intromission. The couple are allowed to enjoy being in sexual contact with penetration of the vagina, but they are told not to proceed to intercourse. They may, of course, reach orgasm.

Finally the couple are allowed to proceed to actual sexual intercourse, and by now they are often relaxed enough to enjoy it with no difficulty. The Masters and Johnson technique is used widely for a whole range of sexual dysfunctions.

Sexual Variations

The last issue that needs mentioning is sexual variations. Some individuals prefer to associate sexual arousal with certain non-sexual experiences. In the past, these have been called deviations, but commentators have argued that in the majority of these desires there is nothing deviant about what is wished, and so there has been a shift of nomenclature and they are now called variations.

The most common sexual variation is the desire, usually of the man, to see his wife clothed in her underwear, in a particular color, which is often black. This is such a common wish that it hardly merits being considered unusual. This fetish, as it is called, moves on to desire the wife or the husband to dress in something smooth, like rubber. There is a whole industry providing men with rubber material. Sometimes the man wants to have intercourse on a rubber sheet. There is no object that cannot be treated as a fetish which is capable of arousing sexual excitement.

Some women find these desires of their husbands acceptable, and there is no moral reason against them. Others object, with the feeling that they are being treated as objects, and that it is the fetish that arouses the husband sexually and not the wife.

Another sexual variation takes the form of wishing to cross-dress during sexual intercourse. The husband wants to dress in female clothes, usually undergarments, and be involved sexually in this way. Cross-dressing does not indicate homosexuality. These are separate conditions. The man who is aroused by cross-dressing is a common entity. These men often tell their partner of this predilection, and women often cooperate with their desire and buy feminine clothing for them, but some find the desire unacceptable and will not cooperate.

The third common variation is sado-masochism. In

this there is a desire for either sex to experience pain, humiliation, or some form of restriction when the sensation desired is masochism, and to inflict them when the need is to be sadistic. Minor forms of sado-masochism are very common, and provided the form taken is acceptable to the couple, there is no harm done. Sado-masochism may take ugly forms and become unacceptable.

All these variations may appear within a marriage, and spouses are variously surprised, astonished, and very uncomfortable, not knowing how to react. When anything beyond ordinary intercourse is asked, it can set off alarm bells. Yet, there is no reason why a couple cannot adapt to a sexual variation that is mutually acceptable. There is no moral objection provided the sexual integrity of the couple is retained.

By far the most common sexual problem in marriage is infidelity, and this is the topic of the next chapter.

15

The Problem of Infidelity

Infidelity is not a new problem. It goes back to biblical times and before, and we have the loving story in the Scriptures when Jesus forgives the woman taken in adultery. Infidelity continues today, and is considered by some to be on the increase, particularly by wives who are trying to catch up with traditional male behavior. There is no doubt that the widespread availability of contraception has made it easier as the fear of pregnancy has receded. It is variously calculated that up to fifty percent of married men and women may indulge in an episode of infidelity. There is evidence that the more promiscuous the person was before marriage, the greater the likelihood that he or she will have extramarital relationships after marriage.

Although all sexual activity outside marriage is treated as infidelity, the nature of these acts varies, constituting different emotional and sexual meanings.

The first category is the one-night stand. Widespread traveling by businessmen and women has made the one-night stand very common. It is a purely physical exchange in which two people who find each other attractive have sex. This act does not deserve the name of making love because there is no personal encounter. Such an encounter does not, of course, threaten the marriage, and there is no intention of leaving the matrimonial home. The main problem is that a venereal disease or AIDS may be caught, and if no precautions are taken pregnancy may ensue, which is often complicated by abortion. The morality of such an act is clear. Sexual intercourse should involve both a personal and sexual dimension, and in this case there is no personal dimension. It is therefore a clear violation of human integrity.

The next type is a transient infidelity which may last for months and sometimes years, in which there is no intention to break up the marriage but insistence on having the extramarital relationship for the time being. These short-term infidelities are also very common, and they can occur with or without the spouse's knowledge. When the affair is discovered, the partner may insist that the liaison be brought to an end, or they may live with it.

The morality of these short-term infidelities concerns the fact that the spouse who is having the affair is devoting time, resources, and feelings that belong to their partner. The other party to the affair is also being cheated of a full relationship. They have to make do with what is left over from the marriage, and it is the married partner who has priority. The spouse is, of course, betrayed, and trust is eroded. In fact everyone is cheated.

The third group of infidelities is when the extramarital relationship is an indication of a serious threat to a marriage that is considered over, and the affair is replacing it.

This is the most serious variety because it often spells the end of the marriage. Frequently the individual is not clear whether the affair is of the second or third variety. This leads to confusion, uncertainty, heated arguments, and great stress. The tension may last a long time as the uncertainty continues. The morality of this type of infidelity is the final betrayal of the spouse.

Why Are People Unfaithful?

If one asks the man or woman in the street why infidelity exists, they would say because of lust, that is, sexual attraction and its allurement. In other words, the popular view is that of hedonism. There is little doubt that sheer physical attraction plays an important role in one-night stand adultery, but that is not the whole story.

Emotions also play a part. The spouse who seeks an extramarital affair of some duration is often seeking an avenue to experience parts of him or herself that are not being realized in the marriage. One of the most common patterns is when the spouse feels that they are not contributing anything of value to the partner and someone comes along who makes them feel needed, appreciated, and wanted. There is a recurrent pattern of a husband or wife relating to a spouse who is apparently self-sufficient and does not need anything from them. Another man or woman comes along who desires emotional attention, and makes the spouse feel that they are needed. This is the form of adultery that acts out a rescue fantasy. Another pattern is the spouse who is in need of emotional and sexual attention. Unconsciously they are looking for what is missing in their life, and when they find someone they pounce.

Another twist to the story is that of the emotionally deprived spouse who never gets enough from their partner and is always looking for extra attention. Such men and women feel excessively deprived, and, whenever they feel recognized, wanted, and appreciated by somebody else, there is the temptation to respond. The maltreated spouse who is seeking solace is easy prey. Alternatively, the spouse may not be fitting the image of their partner. A wife may be married to a husband who is not decisive, strong, dependable. She may long for someone to depend on, and she finds such a person.

Another wife may be married to a husband who is insensitive and is not able to demonstrate feelings. She may long to be held, stroked, and made love to in an affectionate way, and responds to such an overture. Yet another need is that of self-realization. In these circumstances men and women want to assert themselves, and they rebel by having an affair. Commonly an affair is the result of boredom, and the seeking of some excitement, particularly the forbidden, secretive, furtive variety. Such an affair adds to the spice of life.

In all these respects men and women appear to gain something concrete from their experience. Some people maintain that affairs can keep marriages going, and defend them in this light. It is true that both sexes can discover new aspects of themselves in an affair. Commonly they find that their self-esteem rises in the course of the extramarital relationship, and they return to their partner much more assertive and affectionate. They may discover that they are sexually far more interesting than their partner made them feel.

For some people affairs are short cuts to personal enhancement, and undoubtedly something has been gained by the experience. The gain is attained at a price of pain, cheating, betrayal, loss of trust, and the difficulty in maintaining two relationships. Nevertheless the absolute condemnation of infidelity by Christianity fails to grasp that, although the experience is imperfect, infidelity can have positive aspects. Of course, this does not always happen. Disappointment, frustration, pain, and betrayal can also be felt by everyone concerned. Ideally, the positive experience that an affair may give should be striven for and gained within the marriage relationship. But neither society nor the church has reached such a level of understanding of personal relationships to be able to offer the ideal, and so the incomplete and defective form continues.

Attitudes Toward Infidelity

The traditional response to the adulterer has been condemnation with a sense of self-righteousness. This is very common and, of course, totally un-Christian. The genuine Christian response is forgiveness. The person who indicts simply pursues a line of keeping to the rules. This was precisely the position of the Pharisees and Jesus condemned it. An attitude based on the law denies the whole Christian message of love. So we need an approach of forgiveness, even though the relatives and friends are clamoring for blood. There is nothing more difficult than the position of the spouse who wants to forgive, but who is surrounded by a family who wants revenge and divorce. They are saying, "Don't trust him/her. They will do it again."

But in the spirit of the message of this book, we must go beyond forgiveness. It is not enough to take back an erring partner, to be magnanimous, and to humiliate by forgiveness. It is necessary to learn what contributed to the infidelity. Often the faithful spouse is partially responsible for what happened. This interpretation goes against the neat and tidy attitude of those who want black and white situations to condemn and exalt. We have to ask ourselves whether we have been loving and understanding enough, whether we have done justice to

the needs of our spouse, whether we have been emotionally and sexually available, and so on. This is hard
work because the so-called innocent party is being asked
to examine his or her conscience. This sounds unfair.

I am sometimes told, when I take this attitude, that I
am condoning the act of infidelity and trying to find
justification and extenuating circumstances for it. On
the contrary, such an episode is an occasion to learn
something about the marriage as a whole. It is a time
for reflection, and we need to go beyond forgiveness,
particularly if the spouse who has been unfaithful feels
justified by the act.

Problems also arise when the person who is unfaithful
cannot decide whether to return to or leave the marriage.
This is the person who often comes for counseling. One
moment they are at home, and the next with their lover
or mistress. This uncertainty may last for long periods,
causing havoc and deep pain. The uncertainty may be
due to the fact that the home is pulling because of children, obligation, or a sense of guilt, but the heart and attraction remain outside the home. The wife or husband
accepts the spouse back, only for them to leave again.
Skilled counseling is needed to resolve this dilemma.

When the spouse returns home, there may be a clean
break with the third party. This may be a condition for
having the partner back. This clean break is sometimes
achieved, but sometimes not. The actual relationship
with the lover or mistress may have ceased, but feelings
go on and there is an acute desire to know what is happening to the lover. This may lead to complications because letters and telephone calls are continued when
formal promises have been made to cease contact. The
lying is discovered by the spouse, and there are further
recriminations.

Returning is a delicate matter. The feeling that suffers

most is trust. The faithful spouse cannot trust that even a ten-minute delay returning from work is genuine—or has the spouse been unfaithful again? Mistrust can haunt a marriage. This is particularly so when the partner has had problems feeling secure and has anxious attachments. They have lived their whole life with the fear of being abandoned, and now they are facing the possibility directly. It is such men and women who are tormented by infidelity. Their fear becomes a real nightmare. Another element is competition. What has the third party got that the spouse has not?

Fidelity is a basic need for couples. The whole basis of mutual trust depends on it. When the trust is breached, recapturing it takes time, and the original position may never be regained. Faithfulness is a fundamental human need, but the pressures to be unfaithful are great. When it occurs, a couple should use the occasion, as negative as it may be, to examine the state of their relationship, rather than taking condemnatory positions. It is part of genuine loving not only to forgive, but to go beyond forgiveness and try to understand the reasons for it which need repairing.

Ideally all human needs should be met with the chosen relationship, but in practice this is not always possible. Again, ideally there should be constant examination of the ongoing relationship so that deficits can be repaired, but we have not reached the stage when routine assessments of marriages are the order of the day. Sometimes it requires an act of adultery to find out what is missing. When infidelity does take place, there is no reason for divorce. It should be seen as an occasion for deepening the relationship with mutual respect of the partners retained. Jesus forgave the woman taken in adultery, but asked her to sin no more. Couples have to go beyond forgiveness and help each other to sin no more.

16

Parents versus Children

This chapter is not about how to be a good parent (there are plenty of books about that subject) but about the much more difficult challenge of how the parents can remain as a couple, protecting their interests, meeting their own needs in the face of those of their children. Traditionally the Roman Catholic Church has taught that the primary purpose of marriage is the procreation and education of children, and by implication the couple had to subordinate their interests to those of the children. Even without such a teaching, parents are laden with guilt when it comes to deciding between their priorities and those of their children. What is forgotten in all of this is that the best interest of children is for the parents to continue to devote time, affection, and care to each other so that they can generate the energy to look after their children. Counselors hear repeatedly the story of the parent who is so preoccupied with the children that he or she neglects the needs of the spouse. This must be one of the most familiar reasons for marital difficulties. What follows is the briefest outline of an extensive subject.

Triangular Situations

I begin the review of this topic with the familiar story that Freud gave us, namely, that the parent/child relationship is triangular. Freud postulated that the little boy was attracted sexually to mother and wants to displace father from her affection. This is a desire that is cut short by the awareness that father is powerful, and the boy unconsciously fears castration. With this fear he gives up his desire for mother and identifies with the father. This is the famous Oedipus complex which we are all supposed to experience and to resolve by the age of five.

The little girl has a more complicated journey from mother to father and back to mother, which is the Electra complex. There are those who cannot accept the sexual basis of this complex, but would be hard-pressed to deny that there is an emotional closeness between the little boy and mother which has to be transferred to father, and there is an attraction to father by the little girl which has to be transferred to mother. Basically there remains a triangular situation between children and their parents which is very strong, even if not always strictly sexual in nature.

This point is made at the start because there is an inherent splitting and sundering apart of parents by this tendency in children. Young children show preferred affection at times to one parent or another which is reciprocated and can be the cause of tension between parents if they are not aware of this possibility. The same applies to matters of discipline which can split parents wide apart. Children are notoriously capable of playing off one parent against the other by saying "Mommy/ Daddy said I can have this or that, or can do this or that." Parents who are unsure of themselves and lack self-esteem can adjust their behavior to curry favor with their children against the other parent. The rule is that parents must act together, be seen to act together, and appear to be fair.

Time Together

When a baby arrives, there is a real danger that the parents will feel their child comes first at all times. Clearly infants do need constant attention in feeding, changing, and attending to its needs; but as it grows older, there is no doubt that time should be set aside for the couple to go out together. At first leaving the young baby feels like a crime. Parents call the babysitter at frequent intervals to find out how the baby is. They may feel guilty about leaving the child in the care of somebody else. If the babysitter is a grandparent, there is a sense of confidence that the baby is in good hands. There is the constant feeling that no one can look after the child as well as its parents.

Time together is essential for the couple, and they should take one evening a week, if possible, to remind themselves that they are husband and wife. This togetherness is one way of keeping close. There is also the danger that the new baby will become the center of attention, forgetting that spouses have needs and require attention. The incessant preoccupation with the baby can leave one or both parents tired, and there is a danger that between housework and the baby, they will neglect one another.

As children get older, the issue is about putting them to bed early enough so the parents have time together. After all the ploys of one more goodnight story, a glass of water, and going to the bathroom have been exhausted, parents should have time for themselves. The trouble is that by then one or both may be exhausted, and all they want is to go to bed and fall asleep. Nevertheless, time should be made for each other.

Many mothers want to stay at home with their young children until they go to school, but for some this is impossible. They are thus torn between their need to work and their duty to their child. Clearly such a frustrated mother will tense up and convey this stress to the child. The situation eases if the parents are able to find a dependable and trustworthy babysitter or day care center. Some mothers choose to return to work immediately after the birth if there is a good child care situation.

But there is no doubt that parents are often laden with guilt feelings. Whenever their need for time together conflicts with the priority they feel they should give to their children, who are thought to be small, helpless, and dependent, they are worried that if they put themselves first they will permanently damage their child. They should rest assured that their children are far more resilient than they realize and should not feel guilty about taking time for themselves. All these considerations are multiplied when the child is handicapped in some way.

Parents' Sexual Life
I have already described that parents need the sustaining power of sexual intercourse to give them the emotional strength to look after their children. Though sexual intercourse is important while the children are growing up, a series of obstacles which the children pose at various phases of their development have to be overcome.

As babies, they may exhaust the nurturing mother who becomes too tired for sex. Getting up at all hours of the night, coupled with breast feeding, may prove a very tiring combination. Sometimes this combination is reinforced by a post-puerperal depression which puts a woman off sex. Both the tiredness and the depression have to be recognized, and as far as the latter is concerned, attention should be given to treatment if the depression is persistent. For Roman Catholic couples, when the mother is breast feeding and ovulation may take time to return, and they are using the natural methods of birth regulation, special advice should be sought about having intercourse if another baby is not wanted immediately.

As the children grow older there should be a good understanding that the parents do have sexual intercourse, and the goodness and love bonding properties of this act should be freely communicated to the children.

Quarreling and Children

There are parents who feel that any quarrel is bad news and should be avoided at all costs. In particular, it should not take place before the children. This is not the case. Quarreling, when it is not excessive, is a normal attribute of human behavior. Children have feelings of anger, quarrel among themselves, and settle their differences. They should not be surprised to find that their parents have conflicts that need resolution. Quarrels are followed by forgiveness and reconciliation. All this has to be learned, and parents are the best teachers.

But the quarreling should not be a manifestation of naked aggression, physical violence, or bouts caused by excessive alcohol consumption. Many children have memories of seeing or hearing their parents having violent arguments in which someone, usually the mother, was hurt. This is not good for the children.

Sometimes the husband or wife is hurtful physically or emotionally. They may be having an affair, or behaving badly in some other way. Should the distressed parent reveal the unacceptable behavior of the other parent to the children? Children can only too easily be used as a way of attacking an errant spouse, but the good image of the parent should be protected as far as possible. At a certain stage toward the end of the first decade, children know there is something wrong and will ask questions. They should be told the truth, but without vengeance or the desire to blacken the image of the offending parent. At other times, particularly as the children become adolescents, they may make up their own mind and frankly tell one parent or another that they do not respect them. Everything should be done to preserve the image of both parents.

Children rely on both parents to learn values and the meaning of life. Parents should remain a source of trusted respect as long as possible. The other spouse should not use the children to pour out their bitterness. Sexually the children will identify with their own sex parent and get a glimpse of the opposite sex also through their parents. Girls should be growing up with a positive view of men through their fathers, and boys similarly have a good view of girls through their mothers.

It is important that children should get an image of their parents as not being perfect, but *good enough*. They should realize that their parents have limitations and imperfections, but above all that they love their children. A balanced view of imperfection where it exists with loving gives the children the feeling of being loved without idealizing their parents. Children may learn from early on that parents love each other without necessarily approving of all they do, and they, too, can love their parents with discretion about their actions.

Decision Making

Parents naturally make decisions on behalf of their children when they are young, but it is never too early to consult them and give them choices. A three-year-old may be given the choice of what fruit it wants, and in this way learn from an early age to be a responsible person. Later on children should be consulted increasingly, and parents take notice of their decisions. It may come to pass that in such a democracy there may be tensions between what the children want and the desires of the parents. Parents should not systematically sacrifice themselves for their children, but should defer to them when they make a good case for what they want, giving them the feeling that the world is fair.

In general, parents take a great deal of care to meet the needs of their children and to put them first. This is how it should be. Children are dependent creatures and need all the attention they can get, but parents are people in their own right and need to preserve their love and sexuality for each other. Young people have a way of dividing and ruling the household. They should not be allowed to do this. The balance between the requirements of the children and those of the parents is a fine one. The children are best served when the parents do not neglect their own needs.

17

Divorce

Some of the marital difficulties described in these chapters can be negotiated, but some lead to divorce. Divorce has escalated in the whole of Western society since 1960. It is probably the single most important social upheaval in society and has widespread repercussions. At the present moment it is estimated that nearly 50 percent of current marriages are heading for dissolution. In fact the three countries leading the table in divorce are the USA, Russia, and Britain, but all Western societies have high divorce rates.

Why is there such an epidemic of divorce? No one has formulated a clear and precise explanation. What follows are personal observations based on research and interpretation of social changes. I offer three possible reasons.

The first is a global theory and is the most debatable; the second is based on social and psychological findings; and the third is highly personal and has already been described in other chapters.

Global Explanation

Divorce is not a new phenomenon. It was present at the time of Jesus, and it was permitted in Jewish law. The only debate was the grounds for it, which varied between strict conditions to very easy ones. All of this was changed by Jesus' teaching, which argued in favor of permanence. Jesus reverted to a strict indissolubility which has been preserved in all the Western churches, although the Greek Orthodox, Roman Catholic, and Protestant churches respond differently to actual breakdown. The Greek Orthodox church permits second and third marriages on the basis of the economia of grace. The Roman Catholic Church has a very strict definition of indissolubility, namely that a properly consummated sacramental union cannot be dissolved, but has a long history of church tribunals which allow annulments. The Protestant churches vary between strict adherence to considerable flexibility. Nevertheless all these churches adhere to the teaching of Jesus that divorce is an undesirable event, basically inconsistent with the teaching of the New Testament.

As far as the civil law is concerned, the sole ground for divorce today seems to be the irretrievable breakdown of marriage or "irreconcilable differences." Such breakdowns are most often caused by adultery, disruptive behavior, or desertion.

Additional "grounds" are said to poison the subsequent relationship of the couple and the children. So today a "no fault" principle is stressed. Marriage is seen as a relationship, not a contract, and it either survives or it fails. But what is the nature of the relationship and what forces motivate its survival or break-up?

Profound Changes

In the last one hundred and fifty years there have been profound changes in the personal relationships of marriage. Brief references have already been made to these, but are repeated here because they are central to our understanding of divorce. In the early nineteenth century a couple had a life expectancy of about forty or fifty years, and their togetherness was task-oriented. Most couples had to struggle to survive at work and at home. They were busy producing food, keeping warm, and educating their children and keeping them healthy. There was no health insurance or state education, and social support was minimal. The energies of the couple were directed outward toward survival, keeping body and soul together, as they had been for thousands of years before. In the second half of the nineteenth century, education was taken over by the state, relieving the couple of a great deal of responsibility, once again shifting the emphasis from external task-oriented togetherness to an energy-oriented interpersonality.

Despite these changes the couple were still saddled with enormous responsibilities. Traditionally the husband was looked upon as the provider and the woman as the childbearer, rearer, and housekeeper. These were instrumental tasks which survived for a long time, indeed right down to our day, but little by little they are changing. Many wives now work as well, and provisions for the family are often a joint responsibility. Technology has helped to reduce working hours, and offers more leisure and time for togetherness. The progress of medicine has made pregnancy safer, with conception reliable and under the couple's control with contraception. The reduced

family size that has ensued has freed women from a good
deal of child-oriented tasks. Running the household has
become easier, and has also freed spouses for more leisure. More men are slowly (only too slowly!) par-
ticipating in household responsibilities. All this has
changed further the togetherness from external task-
oriented factors to an interpersonal encounter of intimacy.

At the same time as these social changes are happening, two other major events have occurred. The first
is the advent of Freud and dynamic psychology, with a
new emphasis on sexuality, emotions, feelings, and affection, particularly the latter. That is not to say that any of
these features are new; they have always been present.
What is new is the depth of our understanding of them.
Thus the new emotional encounter of couples is im-
pregnated with feelings and emotions that are now in the
forefront of human expectations. Feelings and emotions
are succinctly described under the term "love."

The Emancipation of Women

The second social factor is the emancipation of wom-
en, which has been proceeding for at least two centuries
but has rapidly accelerated in the last thirty years.
Women's emancipation means several things. More
women are bringing verbal ability, communication, and
dealing with feelings to the fore in human relationships
of intimacy. Women's expectations have risen in all these
areas, and men are handicapped in a variety of ways. The
egalitarian relationships required by the emancipation of
women have thrown many men off equilibrium. The new
expectations in demonstrating feelings and communication present special difficulties for men. A good deal of
research is needed in this area. The overall result of wom-
en's emancipation is a basic new man-woman re-

lationship and a much lower tolerance by women of adverse behavior from men, behavior that would have been acceptable in previous generations.

There have thus been major changes in personal relationships, and these changes have all occurred with a rapidity that has given no time for proper assessment, evaluation, and effective educational and supportive measures. The gap between these changes and an effective response in education and in society has been filled by divorce. This has been made easier by two other factors.

The first is that the basic Christian background of Western societies is particularly weak in its understanding and handling of the subjects of sex and women, and despite the fact that sixty to seventy percent of first marriages still take place in church, the churches have proved to be severely impotent in grasping and responding to these changes. Whereas the churches have a long tradition of education and nursing, they have an appalling poverty of thought on sexuality, which has been linked to procreation for two thousand years. Similarly, feelings have been supplanted in the West by reason and the intellect. For these reasons the churches have proved unable to grasp the essentials of change and respond adequately to them. But Christianity has one momentous weapon on its side; its belief that God is love and that human love is a way of exploring divine love. In its recent thought, the main Christian churches have identified the link between marriage and love, and have eloquently described it. What is needed is to put flesh on this insight.

So, if I am right, at the global level the advent of large-scale divorce is due to a rapid transformation from task-oriented togetherness to a personal, emotional encounter which needs different education, social skills, and support. In this respect the Christian community, with its parish-orientation, is one of the remaining visible entities to undertake the work of accurate response and could set the example for the rest of society. It will be argued that this should be one of its principal aims of evangelization. Finally it must be recognized that divorce has become more socially acceptable.

Social and Psychological Factors

Within the overall global transformation I have outlined above, sociologists and psychologists have identified certain characteristics that are related to divorce. The social factors are age, premarital pregnancy, early pregnancy, lack of assortative mating, and social class.

As far as age is concerned, it has been shown repeatedly that marriages in which the partners are under the age of twenty are more likely to break down. It may not be age itself, but the emotional and social immaturity associated with it that is responsible.

Premarital pregnancy and the arrival of a baby in the first few months of marriage have also been shown to be associated with high divorce rates. A pregnancy and the consequent child put constraints on the couple that often lead to resentment and frustration. The combination of youthful marriage and premarital pregnancy creates a particularly adverse situation.

Sociologists have established with some certainty that in the seeking of a partner the field of eligibles is scanned and assortative mating takes place, that is, like marries like. The similarity is in education, social background, age, financial position, race, religion, and generally in social class. There is considerable evidence that, when this similarity is ignored, the risk of divorce rises. There is a common-sense explanation in that the viability of the relationship needs a certain amount of similarity in all these areas. If barriers are crossed in these social factors, there is an added strain that may be the last straw.

When social class is considered, there is a clear inverse relationship between social class and divorce. The highest rates of divorce are found in the lowest socio-economic groups. It is the lowest socio-economic groups that are likely to combine youthful marriages, premarital pregnancy, immaturity, housing, and economic difficulties.

The psychological factors associated with marital breakdown are less clear. Based on the social factors of assortative mating, it was postulated that this would apply to psychological factors and that stable people would marry stable partners, while neurotic ones would be matched by similar neurotic personalities, and that the latter would be more vulnerable. When this hypothesis was put to the test it was found that neurotic men did not marry neurotic women, but, when there was a further assessment a few years later, the women had become equally neurotic!

Thus, we have an explanation, not of assortative mating, but of contaminating interaction. Nevertheless there are strong pointers that marital breakdown is associated markedly with personality disorder. This is not surprising in that both spouses have higher expectations, and this applies particularly to women so that the associated behaviors of aggression, alcoholism, gambling, drug-taking, infidelity, are no longer tolerated as they used to be, particularly when women were dependent on men for their survival.

Personality disorders, which play havoc with marriages, are notoriously confusing entities in psychology and psychiatry. The reason for this is that there are different theoretical frameworks for classification. The first is psychoanalytical, and depends on a dynamic understanding of the growth of the personality. This is largely Freudian and post-Freudian, and has as its base sexuality, aggression, feelings, emotions, affection, and the capacity to form and sustain sexual and emotional relationships. This approach has been immensely productive and modern counseling has been largely derived from dynamic psychology.

The defect in this approach is that a great deal of divorce has been explained on psychological personality grounds, whereas it has been argued in this chapter that the epidemic of divorce is rooted in changing social factors that still have to be addressed. Divorce is much more than psychological pathology, and the danger has been that widespread counseling has unwittingly given the impression that those who divorce are essentially disturbed personalities. Some of them certainly are, but we have failed to discern that what comes first is the surge of emotional intimacy arising from social factors, and only secondly the psychological mechanisms which only partially explain the actual problems. The failure to undertake the social factors is a major defect of psychological thinking, and I, as a psychiatrist, readily admit that I have been as blind as my colleagues.

It can be stated with some certainty that whatever the origins of personality difficulties, the fact is that the personality plays a crucial role in the new dimensions of personal intimacy required by contemporary marriage, and so the only way forward is an interdisciplinary psychosocial approach.

Consequences of Divorce

When the committed Christian approaches such matters as divorce, adultery, and promiscuity, he or she takes a stand based on the teaching of Jesus perpetuated by the church over the last two thousand years. No other measure is needed to claim that divorce is wrong. A great deal of respect is due to this position, but it is not sufficient.

First of all, as a dutiful Christian, it is important to understand in depth the words of Jesus. The Christian faith is based on the wonder of the Old and the New Testaments, particularly the belief that Jesus fulfilled the covenant, and in his own teaching gave us the essentials to understand his Father. We need not only to obey, but to understand why Jesus taught what he did. In this way the mystery of God will be unfolded. Blind obedience, a favorite of many Christians of all denominations, is anathema to an authentic Christian life that rejoices, not in obedience, but in actually living the kingdom of God. Jesus did not make obedience the supreme virtue, but love. In loving, he was actualizing the will of his Father. We have to go beyond obedience to the actualization of Jesus' teaching.

Secondly, in a pluralistic society, Christian teaching cannot be taken for granted. We have to demonstrate that Christian teaching upholds human integrity and can be embraced by the non-Christian because it is authentic. So we have to go beyond proclaiming the gospels. We have to show that gospel values are genuine human values that belong to everybody.

So the questions we have to ask in all moral matters are the human consequences. What are the consequences of contraception, abortion, divorce, adultery, and so on? In our age and time, the Christian truth can only be heard if its veracity is obvious, and that means that the teaching respects human integrity. The same applies to divorce. There are plenty of people who see marriage as a prison in which human distortion, not love, is mobilized. For them, and they littered the landscape in the 60s and 70s, divorce is a liberating experience. So we have to depart from Christian dogma and enter the world of social and psychological consequences. They have to speak in their own right. What follows is a summary of some of the main findings, divided between the impact on the adult and on the children.

Impact on Spouses

Certain things cannot be easily measured. When two people enter a marriage, they promise to love their spouse, and in return be loved back. When this effort fails, there is an inevitable serious knock to their hopes, expectations, trust, and belief in human love. That so many enter into subsequent relationships is a triumph of hope over reality, but there is no denying that every divorce is a nail in the coffin of human love. A divorce is a betrayal of some of the deepest aspirations of the human spirit.

In practice few divorces take place suddenly. Most are preceded by years of conflict and tension, with the consequent symptoms of anxiety, headaches, poor sleep, irritability, depression, tiredness, and lack of energy. It has been estimated that those marital and family tensions are the most common reasons for women to consult a doctor, and for men they come second after work.

As the tension escalates, the episodes of aggression, drinking bouts, and depression become more common, and the whole family is upset, including the children. There are experts who believe that such a global conflict is so damaging that divorce is the best solution. It is true that escalating aggression is damaging, but that is not to say that divorce is a better answer. In fact when the children themselves are questioned they are unequivocal that they want their parents to stay together and resolve their difficulties.

At the time of the separation, there is frequently a host of physical and psychological symptoms that suggest depression. In the immediate post-separation period, the tension and depression are manifested by weeping, in-

creased smoking, drinking, poor sleep, and loss of appetite. Throughout the escalation of marital conflict and
in the post-separation phase, there is an increase in attempted suicides. There is a grieving period after the loss
of the spouse which usually persists for some months,
and occasionally for years. For some, divorce combines
sadness with an accompanying relief that the stress is
over, but many husbands and wives regret divorcing.

After the immediate period of the divorce, what happens to the adults depends on whether they form a subsequent relationship or remain single. There is very
strong evidence that those who remain unattached are
prey to increased psychological illness with much higher
referrals to outpatient departments and admission to psychiatric units. Studies from several countries have shown
that the rate of suicide for the unattached divorcee is
many times higher than for the general population. This
increased tendency to disease applies to physical conditions such as cancer, heart disease, and accidents. Thus
the divorced individual who remains unattached is an infinitely more vulnerable being, physically and psychologically.

A very high percentage of divorced people remarry.
Official figures lately show that remarriage is not so popular, and it has been replaced by cohabitation. We shall
have to wait to see whether the cohabitation phase leads
to marriage. There is common agreement that these second marriages are more likely to break down. In theory,
second marriages ought to be more resilient since the
couple should have learned from the first experience. In
fact, second marriages present problems because the
same intractable characteristics in the personality persist,
the lessons from the first marriage have not been learned,
and the presence of stepchildren adds a great deal of tension. A percentage of subsequent marriages do well, but

what we are all learning is that no contemporary marriage is free from the challenge of interpersonal intimacy, and sustained effort is needed in all marriage relationships.

Impact on Children

In a certain sense, adults are able to look after themselves, even though their experiences are acutely painful. The impact on children is a different matter. Children are dependent on their parents and the atmosphere they create for them. It is beyond dispute that a child prefers to have both parents rather than only one. A good deal of research in the last decade has shown that children do not want their parents to split up, and divorce does have an adverse impact on them. Accumulating evidence shows unequivocally that many, though not all, children suffer as a consequence of divorce.

The National Summary of Children carried out by Furstenberg began in 1976 with 2,274 children between the ages of seven and eleven. In 1981 a sample of 1,428 children was followed up. The study showed that those children who had experienced marital dissolution were significantly worse off than those who had not, with respect to several measures of problem behavior, academic performance, and psychological distress. The most startling finding in this study was that twenty-three percent of the fathers had had no contact with their sons and daughters during the entire preceding year. The researchers conclude that "marital disruption effectively destroys the ongoing relationship between children and the biological parent living outside the home in a majority of families."

I would like to comment on two well-known individual studies: those of 1) Wallerstein and Kelly and 2) Hetherington.

Wallerstein's study consisted of 131 children aged

three to eighteen at the time of separation. The children were followed up to fifteen years. At five years, moderate to severe depression was present in over one-third of the entire original sample. By the ten-year mark a significant number still spoke sorrowfully of their emotional and economic deprivation, and they spoke wistfully of their earlier life within the intact family. Reconciliation fantasies were still discernible in half the sample. At ten years follow-up, the older group ranged from age nineteen to twenty-nine, and they looked back over the post-divorce years with predominant feelings of restrained sadness, resentment at their parents, and a wistful sense of having missed out on growing up in an intact family. A significant number at this stage appeared to be troubled, drifting, and under-achieving. At fifteen years, half of the children were worried, under-achieving, self-deprecating, and sometimes very angry.

The Hetherington sample consisted of 144 well-educated middle-class parents and their children, half of whom were divorced and the other half not. Reports from the immediate aftermath of the legal divorce showed high emotional distress and serious behavioral problems among the children. At the six-year follow-up, by which time the children were ten years old, the data showed that mother-son relationships in the divorced families and the parent-son/daughter relationships in the newly remarried families were all problematic. It is apparent in this study that a significant number of these children who experienced their parents' divorce at age four will enter their adolescence many years later under a severe handicap.

These studies show a remarkable agreement of widespread short-term behavioral disturbances, a long-term social, economic, and psychological disadvantage, with the worst effect of all that children of divorce have a

higher chance ending up divorced themselves, thus in-
stituting a vicious circle.

In 1986, it was calculated that there were one million
one-parent families looking after 1.6 million children.
Every piece of research shows that these one-parent families are seriously economically handicapped, and that the
mother (it is usually the mother) is under stress, over-
tired, harassed, and unable to give due time and attention
to the children, work, and personal life. Undoubtedly
more relief could be given financially, but the strain is
more than an economic one.

Powerful Forces at Work

As we have seen, there are powerful social forces producing historical changes in marriage, coupled with ris-
ing expectations. The gap between these rapid changes
and an effective response has been filled by divorce.
These consequences of divorce are extremely serious, and
it is doubtful whether society or the church has appreciated how serious they are.

It seems to me that, as far as Christianity is concerned,
the changes in marriage and marital breakdown have to
become an urgent priority, eclipsing all other social issues. I have said this before. The reason why I am repeating it is the obvious one, that marriage and the
family are the root of society and the church, and when
they are in distress everything else suffers in consequence.
All we do is spend money and resources to look after disturbed children in schools, sick people in hospitals, de-
linquents in courts, build more public housing for
divorced mothers with children, spend billions to ward
off economic distress, and, above all, create a vicious circle in which the divorced children of today are the divorced parents of tomorrow.

It is astonishing how little importance has been paid

by church leaders, with few exceptions, to this issue. The silence is incomprehensible. I am the last person to deny the pastoral needs of the separated and divorced, but the urgent matter is to have a research program to understand why large-scale divorce is happening. There is no reason for complacency, for the Christian community is not specifically protected from the ravages of marital breakdown. A program of effective research is costly and demanding. The churches have to decide between the priority of education and the family. I have no doubt which should come first, but where is the concerted effort to put the family at the top?

18

The Importance of Counseling

The response to marriage difficulties has been large-scale counseling. While it has proliferated as one of the main answers to marital difficulties, the majority of those who divorce do not use it, and study after study has shown that when people have marital difficulties, they consult first their relatives and friends, and the most common professional they approach is their medical doctor. They often associate marriage counseling with failure, and generally women use it more than men. At the end of this chapter a critique will be offered of marriage counseling, but I want now to consider what happens when marriage counseling is undertaken. No two counselors work in the same way, but some generalizations can be made.

It is much better to see a couple together, but sometimes the husband or wife are seen individually. The remarks that follow apply to the couple being seen to-gether.

When the couple arrive they do not know what to ex-pect. They fear condemnation; they often want the ther-apist to take their side, and to convince the spouse of their erring ways. Above all they want a magical solution. It is important to establish rapport between the therapist and the couple, and to reassure them from the beginning that therapy is not a session of moral judgment, nor a matter of giving advice, although the therapist will be hard-pressed repeatedly for practical solutions to the problems faced.

In practice the therapist encourages the couple to tell their story, each in turn, while the other listens. Interruptions are discouraged, but clarifications are es-sential. Basically the thrust of counseling is to move from the existing paralysis and the tone of mutual crit-icism to establishing what the spouses need from each other which they are not now getting, and why.

The goal of counseling is to go beyond the anger and criticism to mutual needs and to establish why these are not being met. Do spouses really appreciate what the other wants, and what it is that is preventing them from giving and receiving it? The therapist will interpret what the couple need, but if they do not know, an inquiry can be made on the differences at the social, emotional, sex-ual, intellectual, and spiritual levels. Basically, most mar-ital problems surround the issues of sex, affection, availability, and money, and of these affection and sex predominate.

In the course of counseling, a therapist tries not to take sides or to identify with the cause of either husband or wife. Recognition, identification of problems, and fa-cilitation of answers is the counselor's task. Traditionally it is the couple who find the answers, but the counselor is

there to make the task easier. How is this done? At
present there are two basic forms of counseling, the dynamic and the behavioral, and these will be briefly described, not from the point of view of teaching the
method, but for some appreciation of what is involved.

Dynamic Counseling

Dynamic counseling is the most common form used
the world over, and is a derivative of psychoanalytic and
psychotherapeutic processes, although a whole variety of
modifications have taken place.

At the heart of this approach is the basic psycho-
dynamic belief that each individual establishes their personality on the basis of their family interaction with
parents and siblings. The emphasis is on the feelings and
emotions experienced in childhood, and primary attention is paid to anger, love, and sex. In this model, genetic
factors do not play a prominent part. What is stressed is
the pattern of feelings laid down in the first decade of life
that were learned from parents. If there have been trau-
matic, hurtful experiences, and in this model no one es-
capes these entirely, defenses are laid down and they
influence the reaction of the individual. So men and
women emerge from childhood with basic beliefs about
how lovable, wanted, and appreciated they are, with con-
victions about whether they can trust, rely on, expect affirmation from, or be let down by other people.
Childhood is the first experience of emotional intimacy,
and marriage becomes the second experience in which
the spouse will be treated unconsciously with the same
expectations. This is the basic dynamic counseling model
in which men and women marry one another on a basis
of conscious social selection of age, background, education, religion, race, conscious psychological affinity of
what they like and dislike about each other, and un-

conscious emotional collusion, in which the partner is chosen because they resemble or are dissimilar to one or both parents.

When the unconscious characteristics are positive, the spouse is idealized and expected to be loving, affectionate, strong, reliable, generous, understanding, and so on, and the problems begin when they are not. When the unconscious characteristics are negative, the spouse is selected because they repeat the parental features of rejection, criticism, neglect, indifference, and domination. In both instances difficulties arise, and dynamic counseling aims to resolve them.

It does this by rendering conscious what is unconscious, identifying the defenses people use against each other, and moving on to a better understanding of reality by appreciating how their parents actually function and what they have realistically to offer.

There is no doubt that dynamically-based counseling has been immensely productive and rewarding, but it has its limitations. Couples do not easily accept the basis of the model, their unconscious motivation, the need for reality, the hard work that has to go into changing habits of a lifetime, abandoning cherished fantasies, or seeing their spouse in a different light. Dynamic counseling may be able to explain the way of a situation, but it underestimates the effort that is needed to change. Couples may need to be seen for months, sometimes for years. In the traditional dynamic counseling situation, two therapists are recommended, but this is, of course, highly impractical, expensive, and is rarely followed.

Dynamic counseling is effective in the more intellectual, well-motivated couple, and can be most rewarding, but its non-directional, non-interventionist approach has many problems as people expect to be directed, given advice, and they find this approach confusing and difficult to work with. The main theoretical objection with this approach is the belief that all marital problems stem from disturbed childhood experiences, which they do not. This whole approach has failed to appreciate that all marriages are under stress in modern society because of the shift from task-oriented togetherness to an emotional, interpersonal encounter in which dynamic mechanisms play a part, but it is the social changes of intimacy that are the main reasons for the difficulties. The panacea to modern marriage is not more counseling at a late stage, but better education and support for contemporary marriage.

Behavioral Therapy

Some marital therapists became disenchanted with the dynamic model and moved on to an entirely different approach along the lines of behavior psychology, which repudiates the dynamics of the situation and works on totally different principles. Behavioral marital therapy depends on reciprocity negotiation and communication training.

In reciprocity negotiation, there is a simple concept in which it is considered that effective marriages are much more mutually rewarding than troubled ones. In this approach the complaints of the couple are restated in wishes for a change in behavior so as to eliminate the complaints. It is assumed here that there are no unconscious personality clashes, but the couple want more time, sex, empathy, affection, togetherness. In reciprocal negotiation, complaints become wishes, wishes become tasks, tasks are imposed reciprocally, and the carrying out of tasks is monitored by the one who requested them. Of course, for this approach to work what is needed is that the task must be reciprocal, accepted by both partners, be practical, and apply to regularly repeated behavior.

This approach is simple, neat, and effective when there are no underlying emotional and feeling difficulties that make it impossible to carry out the tasks.

The second element of behavior therapy is communication training. A great deal of marital difficulty is due to the failure of couples to understand each other. Effective communication is a key to marital progress, and behavior therapy has some valuable insights that are worth mentioning here.

Couples frequently overgeneralize. For example, an angry husband may say that his wife never does any housework when he means that something specific has been omitted. Spouses generalize and elicit the ire of their partner who simply denies the statement. "So, I never clean the house. How do you think we have lived for the last ten years?"

Clinical observation and investigations have brought to our attention the presence of incongruence. A wife rages at her husband's failure to help at home, and the husband replies ironically, "I agree completely with you, dear." Another example is vague references. The wife says, "All men are after one thing; all they want is sex." The husband feels included in all mankind and begins to protest.

A common problem is impersonal statements. Here the wife or the husband does not ask their partner for a specific request but states, "All men who are genuinely concerned about their home help their wife with the chores." This means: "You are not genuinely concerned about me." This could be put directly, requesting help in the house. Mention has been made of generalization, but it is worth referring to it again. In the course of disputes spouses say to each other: "He/she will never agree. He/she never does anything I want." This generalization needs to be translated into a specific complaint.

Yet another problem comes when one spouse reads the other's mind. "The only reason you are saying this is because you are angry about last night." The wife resents the assumption that her husband knows what is going on inside her. This is an assault on her independence, a domination of her inner world, a presumption about her feelings, and the denial of initiative on her part, in which she is allowed to freely express what she feels. This assumption about the inner world of the spouse also takes place when one spouse says, "We both think X or Y." In both instances the partner may take great delight in telling the spouse they are wrong.

Reciprocity negotiation and communication training are the main planks of behavior therapy, but there are other more sophisticated techniques, designated as structural, using such concepts as boundaries between spouses, their personal territory, dependency, overprotection, enmeshment, symmetry, and complementarity, which involve technicalities we need not bother ourselves with here.

A third approach is dependent on systems theory which is not used very commonly, but has underlying implications for all types of therapy.

Critique of Counseling

Counseling has been available for nearly fifty years, during which period divorce has escalated nearly six hundred percent, and it is therefore pertinent to evaluate it.

In some cases counseling is very useful, but there is a widespread reality that couples do not use it as often as we would expect, and repeated studies show that when in difficulties, they turn to relatives, friends, and their medical doctor for help.

The fact is that after being involved for over thirty years in counseling I have come to recognize some unpalatable facts. Statistics show that couples simply do not use counseling. Men on the whole are more reluctant than women. The majority of couples prefer to sort out their own problems, and associate counseling with failure, both personal and pathological. As far as the couples who are referred to me are concerned, some do very well, but many come too late, having exhausted all hope and motivation, and simply desire a certification of their incompatibility, a view shared by other therapists. All this is disappointing, but it does not mean that counseling must cease or that counselors are not skilled people with a great deal to offer. It means that we have to think afresh how to use this process in a way that is more rewarding.

I believe that we have to recognize that couples must remain motivated to persevere with their marriages. This is a social, religious, and ethical matter. The Christian churches have to reiterate the message about permanency, not as a negative command, but as the realization of the wonderful gift of love. This means that a great deal more attention has to be paid to marriage as a source of fulfillment of human potential. Coupled with this positive attitude, we must come to appreciate the damage that marital breakdown inflicts on the children and the spouses, particularly the former. When this subject is mentioned, there is the fear that all we shall do is inculcate guilt in those who are divorced or divorcing. The result has been that in some quarters, divorce has been made to look reasonable, not damaging, and a very rational approach to modern reality. It is imperative that both society and the church face realistically that marriage is in the throes of historic change, which presents a major challenge. The point is not to make people feel guilty, but to raise collective awareness and responsibilities.

I am suggesting that the way forward is to move from

a program of counseling at a late stage to "prevention," intervening at much earlier stages when the couple still has hope and motivation to persevere in the relationship. This means that we have to work in our schools and churches to prepare for marriage and to offer support after the wedding. We need to look at prevention as the major instrument of support for marriage, placing in the hands of the couple the means of pursuing their own destiny. The churches have to become communities of love that facilitate marriage. They need to support couples at a much earlier stage, and help them to review and assess their marriage at regular intervals. Pastorally we have to move from seeing the wedding as the conclusion of the church's involvement to being the beginning. We need to support couples throughout their married cycle.

19

Contemporary Loving

This book has attempted to examine the internal shift of marriage from an institution for the begetting and raising of children to primarily an interpersonal relationship of love of the spouses, out of which the energy for conceiving and educating the children will rise. We are in the midst of this change, and we need to understand and appreciate it in depth if we are to reduce the colossal damaging impact of marital breakdown.

In the past, marriage was seen primarily to be for children and the energy of the spouses to be expended in raising them. Their interpersonal relationship was of secondary importance. Their togetherness was action-oriented in structuring a partnership of the man to be the center of action as a provider and head of the family, and the wife as a begetter and raiser of children. This inner world of marriage focused on children, and the time before their arrival and after their departure was hazy. The relationship of the couple was subordinate to the needs of the children.

Within this framework of marriage, the difficulties that arose in the marriage were largely understood as an expression of selfishness. This traditional view is expressed to this very day, as evil is fully understood by the egoism of the people concerned. The selfishness was further explained by lack of self-control, and in sexual matters as lack of suppression of instincts. Suppression was the normal order of the day. Between them, control and suppression dictated all conduct and behavior. Things were not talked through, they were controlled. Anger, violence, and sex drives were all to be suppressed. This applied directly to sexual matters, which were a particular object of suppression.

When things went wrong, the way to change them was by allocating wrongdoing on one partner or the other, accepting blame, and seeking forgiveness. The supreme Christian weapon was to forgive the guilty party. An essential part of understanding human relationships was the need to find a "bad" and "good" spouse and allocate badness and goodness respectively. There was no point beyond forgiveness except to tolerate what could not be changed. This attitude was reinforced by the popular belief that people could not change, and there was no point in trying to alter or expect change in one's spouse. Spouses settled for compromise and did not, except on rare occasions, proceed to divorce or separation.

If we are to understand what is happening to marriage today, we have to accept that all these traditional values are in the process of being altered. As we have seen throughout this book, marriage is changing from an in-

stitution largely devoted to raising children to an interpersonal relationship of intimacy, in which couples seek
the realization of their potential and maximum fulfillment of feelings and sexuality. Children are raised and
nurtured, but the strength of their total education is being derived from the interpersonal energy sustained by
the relationship. There is a good deal of tension between
the priorities of the interpersonal relationship and the
needs of the children.

The emphasis on the interpersonal relationship stems
from the breakdown of clearly delineated roles of the
spouses to a world in which women are covering many of
the same areas as men. This has shifted the world of men
and women from togetherness based on action to intimacy based on availability, communication, and feelings. In this shift, men have suffered from a loss of
closely delineated roles, and have been invited to enter
the woman's world of words and feelings, in which the
latter has distinct advantages. Loving here has shifted
from action to quality of relationship, and there is an emphasis on sustaining, healing, and growth.

The traditional answer to marital difficulties of selfishness is giving way to a desire to be understood psychologically. Why am I behaving in this way? Why are you
behaving in that way? Men and women are hungry to be
understood and to be responded to accurately instead of
being dismissed as "bad." A hundred years of psychology
of all types, but particularly the dynamic variety, have
transformed human horizons. Instead of being indicted,
spouses long to be reached in the depths of their being,
and to be helped in as many ways as possible to realize
their potential. Dynamic psychology has made us aware
that there is a reason for our behavior. We want to find
the reasons for our behavior and be helped to overcome
the difficulties. We long to be healed and to grow. We

long to have our origins appreciated, our vulnerabilities recognized, respected, and possibly remedied.

In the past the best that we could hope for was to be humble enough, acknowledge our faults, and ask to be forgiven, but at the moment of forgiveness we remained labeled as guilty. It was the magnanimity of our spouse that forgave us. Modern men and women know enough of psychology to appreciate that their behavior is, up to a point, determined, and they are not as responsible as their indicters would like to make them. They long for a human relationship that goes beyond human forgiveness to the restoration of their human integrity. They long for their spouse to understand them and to help them be restored to a fuller sense of their potential. They do not want to be stuck with a magnanimous spouse who "forgives" but retains superiority over them.

Contemporary spouses have higher expectations of each other. In particular, women expect so much more from men. These high expectations are here to stay. They are a permanent feature of the fabric of the man-woman encounter. Theologically, instead of being seen as unrealistic feminist aspirations, they can be considered as the quest of both sexes for a realization of the image of God, not by denial and limitations, but by a plenitude of being.

In this quest, sacrifice is needed. This is where Christianity can make a specific contribution. Healing and growth cannot be achieved in a moment. They take a lifetime of achievement, but sacrifice now is not a static entity. It is no longer acquiescence to the inevitable. Sacrifice is required to pursue in depth the personality of the partner, and to help them overcome their difficulties. Instead of dismissing one's spouse, spouses want to be helped to deepen their personality. Sacrifice is the equivalent of the patience of the therapist who waits and helps the patient to change.

Spouses are no longer prepared to put up with impossible spouses. Of course, it all depends on what is interpreted as an "impossible" spouse. Western societies have to learn that, by giving up one spouse they are not buying a ticket to heavenly bliss with the next partner. They are right in insisting on change, but loving implies a prolonged period of waiting in which there is active change, and they have a role to play in that change by encouraging, affirming, and praising efforts a partner makes to change.

Spouses want to change the traditional concept of "putting up" with unacceptable behavior. They want to minimize what they "put up" with. The whole ethos of contemporary human relationship is a realization of human integrity, not a denial and suppression of the unacceptable. Christianity can only rejoice at this quest for wholeness. It needs to show that loving is not achieved by denial and suppression but by a lifetime exploration whereby behavior can be changed. The aim is to change positively here on earth. This means that Christians have to emphasize this world as a place of human perfection, and not to treat it as a vale of tears. Human beings are hungry for perfection here and now, and their biggest opportunity to realize it is in their interpersonal relationships.

To sum up, we are witnessing a phase in human relationships in which men and women are seeking human integrity in the presence of each other. Being understood and responded to accurately is the key to loving. At its best Christianity teaches couples to forgive and accept the limitations of a spouse. This is superb, but it is no longer enough. We have to take heed of the teaching of our Lord, who coupled forgiveness with the injunction "sin no more." Sinning no more is realizing one's potential and integrity. Spouses are anxious to learn about their potential and integrity from each other. They want their partner to understand them and facilitate their healing and growth. That is why we have to impart to our children a deeper insight as to how men and women function, so that in the depths of their intimacy, they can reach out to the hurt child in each other and heal it.

Loving implies a process of never-ending healing and growth, and there cannot be any finer goal for Christian spirituality. There has to be a fundamental shift in Christian thought from explaining everything in terms of selfishness to a genuine understanding of the needs of the other and responding to them.

All this applies to interpersonal love, but we must also appreciate that there has been a radical shift in sexuality. For nearly two thousand years sex has been tied to procreation. It has to be realized that that era is over. Sexual intercourse is now unequivocally an expression of love, combining the erotic with the personal. Christianity has to embrace this point of view. It has no difficulty in understanding the importance of personal love, but it must take the plunge and rejoice in the erotic. Then it can help society realize that the fullness of sexuality is to be found in the conjunction between the erotic and the personal. The world is besotted with the erotic but is not so strong on personal love, and there is much emphasis on the transient realization of pleasure.

Christianity, which has a weak grasp of the momentous importance of the erotic, plays it down and tries to emphasize personal love. In the past it emphasized procreation. It is necessary for the erotic and the personal to join forces and become mutually significant. Christianity has to appreciate that sexual instincts are not to be suppressed, but confined to personal loving, and society has to realize that unfettered

sexual instincts do not represent authentic human behavior. In this way lack of self-esteem is translated into
fullness of being and self-esteem.

Christianity has to recognize the shifts in the internal
world of marriage from children to spouses, from a pa-
triarchal point of view to an equality of the sexes, from a
togetherness based on activity and social roles, to an intimacy of love.

Our challenge is to move beyond the first halting steps
of understanding marriage as a community of love to actually fleshing out what that love is in terms of interpersonal needs and sexuality. If we do this in our schools,
churches, and communities, a new dawn of Christian
marriage will emerge in which the domestic church and
evangelization will be its manifestation, and a new spring
of love will emerge from the ashes of marital breakdown
and divorce.

Of Related Interest...

On Life and Love
A Guide to Catholic Teaching on Marriage and Family
William Urbine and William Seifert

A concise reference work summarizing the key documents of the Roman Catholic Church on marriage and family life. The authors define these statements in terms of historical relevance as well as applicability today.
                                        ISBN: 0-89622-570-4, 128 pp, $12.95

A Decision to Love
A Marriage Preparation Program
John M.V. Midgley and Susan Vollmer Midgley

This program is based on the realization that in a world of complex relationships, couples need to love with their heads as well as with their hearts. Exercises and questions help couples explore their feelings. (Leader's guide also available.)   ISBN: 0-89622-514-3, 128 pp, $6.50

Ecumenical Marriage and Remarriage
Gifts and Challenges to the Churches
Michael Lawler

The author challenges churches to recognize the gift of grace inherent in couples involved in ecumenical marriages and in remarriages.
                                        ISBN: 0-89622-441-4, 112 pp, $8.95

Making Your Marriage Work
Growing in Love After Falling in Love
Christopher C. Reilly

This book looks at marriage from a positive, growth-oriented perspective, emphasizing communication, accommodation and acceptance as cornerstones for building a strong marital bond.   ISBN: 0-89622-387-6, 164 pp, $7.95

Secular Marriage, Christian Sacrament
Michael Lawler

This book seeks to uncover the very essence of Christian marriage, an essence that resides in the faith of the baptized, believing couple. It examines the distinction between secular marriage and Christian sacrament, recognizing that each exists in response to specific needs. ISBN: 0-89622-273-x, 140 pp, $8.95

Available at religious bookstores or from

TWENTY-THIRD PUBLICATIONS
P.O. Box 180 • Mystic, CT 06355
1-800-321-0411